Step Forward

Languag for Everyday Life

SERIES DIRECTOR
Jayme Adelson-Goldstein

Includes
Student Audio CD

4 Barbara R. Denman

OXFORD
UNIVERSITY PRESS

OXFORD
UNIVERSITY PRESS

198 Madison Avenue
New York, NY 10016 USA

Great Clarendon Street, Oxford OX2 6DP UK

Oxford University Press is a department of the University of Oxford.
It furthers the University's objective of excellence in research, scholarship,
and education by publishing worldwide in

Oxford   New York

Auckland Cape Town Dar es Salaam Hong Kong Karachi
Kuala Lumpur Madrid Melbourne Mexico City Nairobi
New Delhi Shanghai Taipei Toronto

With offices in

Argentina Austria Brazil Chile Czech Republic France Greece
Guatemala Hungary Italy Japan Poland Portugal Singapore
South Korea Switzerland Thailand Turkey Ukraine Vietnam

OXFORD and OXFORD ENGLISH are registered trademarks of
Oxford University Press

© Oxford University Press 2008

Database right Oxford University Press (maker)

Library of Congress Cataloging-in-Publication Data
Step Forward : English for everyday life.
  p. cm.
  Step Forward 3 by Jane Spigarelli;
  Step Forward 4 by Barbara R. Denman.
  ISBN: 978-0-19-439226-6 (3 : pbk.)
  ISBN: 978-0-19-439227-3 (4 : pbk.)
  1. English language—Textbooks for foreign students. 2. English language–
Problems, exercises, etc. III. Spigarelli, Jane. IV. Denman, Barbara R.
PE1128.S2143 2006
428.2'4—dc22

2006040090

No unauthorized photocopying

Executive Publisher: Janet Aitchison
Editorial Manager: Stephanie Karras
Editor: Glenn Mathes II
Associate Editor: Olga Christopoulos
Art Director: Maj-Britt Hagsted
Senior Designer: Michael Steinhofer
Senior Art Editor: Judi DeSouter
Art Editor: Robin Fadool
Production Manager: Shanta Persaud
Manufacturing Controller: Eve Wong

Student Book ISBN: 978 0 19 439227 3
Student Book with CD-ROM pack ISBN: 978 0 19 439656 1
Student Book as pack component ISBN: 978 0 19 439661 5
Audio CD-ROM as pack component ISBN: 978 0 19 439666 0

Printed in China
20 19 18

This book is printed on paper from certified and well-managed sources.

The publishers would like to thank the following for their permission to adapt
copyright material:
p. 14-15 "Test Anxiety" used with permission of www.hsc.edu
p. 14-15 "Managing Test Anxiety" used with permission of SDS's Learning Skills
Services, The University of Western Ontario web site, www.sdc.uwo.ca
p. 28-29 "News Audiences Increasingly Politicized: Where Americans Go for News"
used with permission of http://people-press.org
p. 42-43 "Background on CTIA's Semi-Annual Wireless Industry Survey" used with
permission of CTIA - The Wireless Association®
p. 56 "Career Exploration" used with permission of www.acinet.org
p. 168-169 Copyright © 2002 by The New York Times Co. Adapted from "She has a
Knife and She Knows How to Use it", by Elaine Louie, originally published June 5,
2002 by The New York Times

ACKNOWLEDGMENTS

Cover photograph: Corbis/Punchstock
Back cover photograph: Brian Rose

Illustrations by: Jane Spencer, p.2, p.8, p.36, p.101, p.134; Bill Dickson, p.3, p.25, p.34,
p.53, p.67, p.107, p.138, p.165,;Tom Newscom, p.4, p.116, p.158; Karen Minot, p.5,
p.19, p.61, pg.102 (#'s 2, 3, and 4), p.144; John Batten, p.6, p.13 (top), p.55, p.64,
p.78, p.110, p.111, p.123, p.148, p.151; Geo Parkin, p.11, p.23, p.40, p.74, p.96, p.112,
p.124, p.130, p.154, p.155; Annie Bissett, p.13, (bottom), p.28, p.69 (bottom), p.139
(top), p.162; Arlene Boehm, p.17, p.20, p.24, p.39, p.125; Barb Bastian, p.18, p.47,
p.70, p.81, p.89, p.109, p.117, p.125, p.137, p.145, p.159; Laurie Conley, p.31, p.45,
p.46, p.92, pg.102 (#'s 5, 6, 7, 8, and 9), p.120, p.143, p.157; Uldis Klavins, p.32, p.60;
Mark Hannon, p.33, p.75; Shawn Banner, p.50; Terry Paczko, p.88, p.95; Ken Dewar,
p.103; Kevin Brown, p.106, p.126, Mike Hortens, p. 75, p.83, p.131, p.139, p.153.

We would like to thank the following for their permission to reproduce photographs:
Photo Edit Inc.: Spencer Grant, p.10; Index Stock: HIRB, p.14; Getty Images: Don
Emmert, p.18 (General Assembly); Punch Stock: p.19 (bus); Photo Edit Inc.: Michael
Newman, p.19 (traffic); Age Fotostock: Grantpix, p.22; Age Fotostock: Andy Goodwin,
p.38; Punch Stock/Digital Vision: p.42 (man); Punch Stock: p.42 (woman); Getty
Images: Mecky, p.52 (american sights); Punch Stock/Visions of American.com: Joseph
Sohm, p.52 (football game); Photo Edit Inc.: Kayte M. Deioma, p.59; Reuters: p.66;
Photo Edit Inc.: Spencer Grant, p.69 (teacher); Age Fotostock: Michael N. Paras, p.69
(hotel worker); Masterfile: Dana Hursey, p.69 (computer technician); Photo Edit Inc.:
Barbara Stitzer, p.73; Masterfile: p.84; Superstock/BrandX: p.87; Superstock: Nicholas
Eveleigh, p.94 (computer); Superstock/SSC: p.94 (books); The Image Works: Lauren
Goodsmith, p.98; Punch Stock: p.102; Masterfile: Jeremy Maude, p.108; Masterfile:
p.115 (left); Getty Images: Marc Romanelli, p.115 (right); Photo Edit Inc.: Dana White,
p.129; Photo Edit Inc.: Tony Freeman, p.136 (top); Photo Edit Inc.: Cindy Charles,
p.136 (bottom); Masterfile: Tim Mantoani, p.144; Dennis Kitchen: Masterfile:
Steven Puetzer, p.153; Superstock/Banana Stock: p.159; Photo Edit Inc.: p.164 (top);
Masterfile: p.164 (bottom); Photo Edit Inc.: Sonda Dawes, p.168; Getty Images: Ryan
McVay, p.171.

We gratefully acknowledge the gifted *Step Forward Book 4*
editorial and design team: Stephanie Karras, Meg Brooks, Amy
Cooper, Glenn Mathes, Ellen Northcutt, Maj-Britt Hagsted,
Michael Steinhofer, and Robin Fadool. We also thank our
students, colleagues and teachers for their inspiration along
the way.

Barbara Denman
Jayme Adelson-Goldstein

Many thanks to Jayme, and to Amy and Jane, for everything.
This book is for my family, and especially for my parents,
Shirley and Harry Denman, with thanks for their true gifts of
patience and support.

–Barbara

I am deeply thankful that Barbara agreed to bring her excellent
and insightful teaching to this series. This book is dedicated
to Stephanie, whose zest for life and work makes her a joy to
know.

–Jayme

ACKNOWLEDGMENTS

The Publisher and Series Director would like to acknowledge the following individuals for their invaluable input during the development of this series:

Vittoria Abbatte-Maghsoudi Mount Diablo Unified School District, Loma Vista Adult Center, Concord, CA

Karen Abell Durham Technical Community College, Durham, NC

Millicent Alexander Los Angeles Unified School District, Huntington Park-Bell Community Adult School, Los Angeles, CA

Diana Allen Oakton Community College, Skokie, IL

Bethany Bandera Arlington Education and Employment Program, Arlington, VA

Sandra Bergman New York City Department of Education, New York, NY

Chan Bostwick Los Angeles Technology Center, Los Angeles, CA

Diana Brady-Herndon Napa Valley Adult School, Napa, CA

Susen Broellos Baldwin Park Unified School District, Baldwin Park, CA

Carmen Carbajal Mitchell Community College, Statesville, NC

Jose Carmona Daytona Beach Community College, Daytona Beach, FL

Ingrid Caswell Los Angeles Technology Center, Los Angeles, CA

Joyce Clapp Hayward Adult School, Hayward, CA

Beverly deNicola Capistrano Unified School District, San Juan Capistrano, CA

Edward Ende Miami Springs Adult Center, Miami Springs, FL

Gayle Fagan Harris County Department of Education, Houston, TX

Richard Firsten Lindsey Hopkins Technical Education Center, Miami, FL

Elizabeth Fitzgerald Hialeah Adult Center, Hialeah, FL

Mary Ann Florez Arlington Education and Employment Program, Arlington, VA

Leslie Foster Davidson Mitchell Community College, Statesville, NC

Beverly Gandall Santa Ana College School of Continuing Education, Santa Ana, CA

Rodriguez Garner Westchester Community College, Valhalla, NY

Sally Gearhart Santa Rosa Junior College, Santa Rosa, CA

Norma Guzman Baldwin Park Unified School District, Baldwin Park, CA

Lori Howard UC Berkeley, Education Extension, Berkeley, CA

Phillip L. Johnson Santa Ana College Centennial Education Center, Santa Ana, CA

Kelley Keith Mount Diablo Unified School District, Loma Vista Adult Center, Concord, CA

Blanche Kellawon Bronx Community College, Bronx, NY

Keiko Kimura Triton College, River Grove, IL

Jody Kirkwood ABC Adult School, Cerritos, CA

Matthew Kogan Evans Community Adult School, Los Angeles, CA

Laurel Leonard Napa Valley Adult School, Napa, CA

Barbara Linek Illinois Migrant Education Council, Plainfield, IL

Alice Macondray Neighborhood Centers Adult School, Oakland, CA

Ronna Magy Los Angeles Unified School District Central Office, Los Angeles, CA

Jose Marlasca South Area Adult Education, Melbourne, FL

Laura Martin Adult Learning Resource Center, Des Plaines, IL

Judith Martin-Hall Indian River Community College, Fort Pierce, FL

Michael Mason Mount Diablo Unified School District, Loma Vista Adult Center, Concord, CA

Katherine McCaffery Brewster Technical Center, Tampa, FL

Cathleen McCargo Arlington Education and Employment Program, Arlington, VA

Todd McDonald Hillsborough County Public Schools, Tampa, FL

Rita McSorley Northeast Independent School District, San Antonio, TX

Gloria Melendrez Evans Community Adult School, Los Angeles, CA

Vicki Moore El Monte-Rosemead Adult School, El Monte, CA

Meg Morris Mountain View Los Altos Adult Education District, Los Altos, CA

Nieves Novoa LaGuardia Community College, Long Island City, NY

Jo Pamment Haslett Public Schools, East Lansing, MI

Liliana Quijada-Black Irvington Learning Center, Houston, TX

Ellen Quish LaGuardia Community College, Long Island City, NY

Mary Ray Fairfax County Public Schools, Springfield, VA

Tatiana Roganova Hayward Adult School, Hayward, CA

Nancy Rogenscky-Roda Hialeah-Miami Lakes Adult Education and Community Center, Hialeah, FL

Lorraine Romero Houston Community College, Houston, TX

Edilyn Samways The English Center, Miami, FL

Kathy Santopietro Weddel Northern Colorado Literacy Program, Littleton, CO

Dr. G. Santos The English Center, Miami, FL

Fran Schnall City College of New York Literacy Program, New York, NY

Mary Segovia El Monte-Rosemead Adult School, El Monte, CA

Edith Smith City College of San Francisco, San Francisco, CA

Alisa Takeuchi Chapman Education Center Garden Grove, CA

Leslie Weaver Fairfax County Public Schools, Falls Church, VA

David Wexler Napa Valley Adult School, Napa, CA

Bartley P. Wilson Northeast Independent School District, San Antonio, TX

Emily Wonson Hunter College, New York, NY

TABLE OF CONTENTS

Listening & Speaking	CASAS Life Skills Competencies	Standardized Student Syllabi/ LCPs	SCANS Competencies	EFF Content Standards
• Listen for and give personal information • Talk about a variety of topics with a partner	0.1.2, 0.1.4, 0.1.5, 0.2.1, 7.4.5	39.01, 49.09, 49.10, 50.02	• Listening • Speaking • Sociability	• Listening actively • Speaking so others can understand
• Talk about personality traits • Discuss personal learning styles • Discuss issues about learning English • Listen to a conversation about educational topics • Discuss test-taking issues **Grammar listening:** • Listen for action or non-action verbs **Pronunciation:** • "t" sound	**L1:** 0.1.2, 0.1.5, 0.2.1, 4.8.1, 7.4.5 **L2:** 0.1.2, 0.1.5, 0.2.1, 0.2.3, 7.4.7, 7.4.9 **L3:** 0.1.2, 0.2.1, 7.4.7 **L4:** 0.1.2, 0.1.5, 0.2.1, 1.1.3, 1.1.8, 6.0.3, 6.0.4, 6.1.4, 6.7.2 **L5:** 0.1.2, 0.1.5, 0.2.1, 2.5.6, 7.4.4, 7.4.9 **RE:** 0.1.2, 0.1.5, 0.2.1, 4.8.1, 7.3.1, 7.3.2, 7.3.4, 7.4.9	**L1:** 39.01, 49.02, 49.10, 49.16 **L2:** 39.01, 49.02, 49.13, 49.16, 49.17 **L3:** 49.16, 49.17, 50.02 **L4:** 39.01, 49.02, 49.03, 49.09 **L5:** 39.01, 49.06, 49.16, 49.17 **RE:** 39.01, 49.01, 49.13, 49.16, 49.17, 50.02	Most SCANS are incorporated into this unit, with an emphasis on: • Knowing how to learn • Participating as a member of a team • Seeing in the mind's eye	Most EFFs are incorporated into this unit, with an emphasis on: • Conveying ideas in writing • Reading with understanding • Reflecting and evaluating
• Talk about news habits • Discuss a current event from the news • Listen to a conversation about a current event • Listen to a news story • Discuss issues related to controversial news **Grammar listening:** • Listen for sentences with the same meaning **Pronunciation:** • Stressing words to clarify meaning	**L1:** 0.1.2, 0.1.5, 0.2.1, 4.8.1, 7.4.4 **L2:** 0.1.2, 0.1.5, 7.2.1, 7.4.4 **L3:** 0.1.2, 0.1.5, 7.2.1, 7.4.4 **L4:** 0.1.2, 0.1.5, 0.2.1, 6.0.3, 6.0.4, 6.1.2, 7.4.4 **L5:** 0.1.2, 0.1.5, 0.2.1, 7.4.4 **RE:** 0.1.2, 0.1.5, 0.2.1, 4.8.1, 7.2.4, 7.3.1, 7.3.2, 7.3.4	**L1:** 38.01, 39.01, 49.02, 49.09 **L2:** 49.02, 49.03, 49.13, 49.16 **L3:** 0.1.2, 0.1.5, 7.2.1, 7.4.4 **L4:** 39.01, 49.02, 49.09, 49.16, 49.17 **L5:** 39.01, 49.02, 49.16, 49.17 **RE:** 39.01, 49.02, 49.16	Most SCANS are incorporated into this unit, with and emphasis on: • Knowing how to learn • Participating as member of a team • Speaking	Most EFFs are incorporated into this unit, with an emphasis on: • Convey ideas in writing • Listen actively • Read with understanding
• Talk about traveling and travel emergencies • Discuss feelings about speaking English on the phone • Listen to an automated message • Talk about cell phones **Grammar listening:** • Listen and complete sentences with reported speech **Pronunciation:** • The letter "s"	**L1:** 0.1.2, 0.1.5, 0.2.1, 2.5.1, 4.8.1, 7.2.5, 7.4.5, 7.4.7 **L2:** 0.1.2, 0.1.5, 0.2.1, 7.4.7, 7.5.6 **L3:** 0.1.2, 0.1.5, 0.2.1 **L4:** 0.1.2, 0.1.5, 0.2.1, 2.2.1, 6.0.3, 6.0.4, 6.2.1, 6.2.3, 6.2.5 **L5:** 0.1.2, 0.1.5, 0.2.1, 2.1.4, 7.4.4, 7.4.7 **RE:** 0.1.2, 0.1.5, 0.2.1, 4.8.1, 7.3.1, 7.3.2, 7.3.4	**L1:** 39.01, 44.01, 49.02, 49.03, 49.10, 49.17 **L2:** 39.01, 49.01, 49.02, 49.03, 49.16, 49.17 **L3:** 39.01, 49.09, 49.13, 50.07 **L4:** 39.01, 40.02, 43.02, 43.04, 49.02, 49.09, 51.03 **L5:** 39.01, 49.02, 49.04, 49.09, 49.16, 49.17 **RE:** 39.01, 49.01, 49.02, 49.16	Most SCANS are incorporated into this unit, with and emphasis on: • Creative thinking • Reading • Speaking	Most EFFs are incorporated into this unit, with an emphasis on: • Conveying ideas in writing • Observing critically • Speaking so others can understand

Listening & Speaking	CASAS Life Skills Competencies	Standardized Student Syllabi/ LCPs	SCANS Competencies	EFF Content Standards
• Talk about future work plans • Discuss career centers and job preparation • Talk about resumes • Listen to a conversation about a resume • Discuss best ways to find jobs **Grammar listening:** • Listen for information using the past perfect **Pronunciation:** • Use rising intonation to check understanding	L1:0.1.2, 0.1.5, 0.2.1, 4.1.4, 4.4.2, 4.4.5, 4.8.1, 7.4.5 L2: 0.1.2, 0.1.5, 0.2.3, 4.1.2, 7.4.7 L3: 0.1.2, 0.1.5, 0.2.1, 7.4.7 L4: 0.1.2, 0.1.5, 0.2.1, 4.1.5, 6.0.3, 6.0.4, 6.1.1, 6.6.6, 7.4.7, 7.5.6 L5: 0.1.2, 0.1.5, 2.5.6, 4.1.9, 7.4.4, 7.4.7 RE:0.1.2, 0.1.5, 0.2.1, 4.8.1, 7.2.4, 7.3.1, 7.3.2, 7.3.4	L1: 37.01, 39.01, 35.03, 49.10 L2: 49.02, 49.13, 49.16, 49.17 L3: 39.01, 49.01, 49.02, 49.16, 49.17, 50.02 L4:39.01, 49.02, 49.09, 49.16, 49.17, 51.05 L5:35.04, 38.01, 49.04, 49.09, 49.16, 49.17 RE:35.03, 39.01, 49.01, 49.02, 49.13	Most SCANS are incorporated into this unit, with an emphasis on: • Arithmetic/Mathematics • Decision making • Interpreting and communicating information	Most EFFs are incorporated into this unit, with an emphasis on: • Cooperating with others • Observing critically • Taking responsibility for learning
• Talk about safety and warning signs • Talk about weather emergencies and emergency plans • Listen to a conversation about reporting an unsafe situation • Listen to a news story about different jobs • Discuss dangers in the home and workplace **Grammar listening:** • Listen for sentences with the same meaning **Pronunciation:** • "ough" words	L1: 0.1.2, 0.1.5, 3.4.1, 3.4.2, 4.3.1, 4.8.1, 7.4.5 L2: 0.1.2, 0.1.5, 0.2.1, 2.3.3, 3.4.2, 7.4.2, 7.4.7 L3: 0.1.2, 0.1.5, 7.4.7 L4: 0.1.2, 0.1.5, 4.3.4, 6.7.4, 7.4.7L5: 0.1.2, 0.1.5, 3.4.2, 7.4.4 RE: 0.1.2, 0.1.5, 0.2.1, 3.4.2, 4.8.1, 7.3.1, 7.3.2	L1:36.03, 44.01, 49.10, 49.16 L2: 44.01, 49.02, 49.16, 49.17 L3: 44.01, 49.01, 49.02, 49.09, 49.13, 49.16, 49.17 L4:36.03, 44.01, 49.02, 49.09, 49.16, 49.17 L5: 38.01, 44.01, 49.02, 49.09, 49.16, 49.17 RE: 39.01, 44.01, 49.01, 49.13, 49.16, 49.17	Most SCANS are incorporated into this unit, with an emphasis on: • Acquiring and evaluating information • Organizing and marinating information • Problem solving	Most SCANS are incorporated into this unit, with an emphasis on: • Acquiring and evaluating information • Organizing and marinating information • Problem solving
• Talk about useful skills for different situations • Listen to conversations to determine workplace hierarchy • Listen to an automated phone menu • Discuss the importance of good interpersonal skills **Grammar listening:** • Listen to and match main clauses with adjective clauses **Pronunciation:** • Saying *yes* and *no* in informal situations	L1: 0.1.2, 0.1.5, 0.2.1, 4.1.7, 4.4.1, 4.6.1, 4.8.1, 7.4.5 L2: 0.1.2, 0.1.5, 0.2.1, 4.6.2 L3: 4.6.5, 7.4.7 L4: 0.1.2, 0.1.5, 4.2.1, 6.0.3, 6.0.4, 6.0.5, 6.1.2 L5: 0.1.2, 0.1.5, 4.4.1, 4.8.7, 7.4.4, 7.5.6 RE: 0.1.2, 0.1.5, 0.2.1, 7.2.6, 7.3.1, 7.3.2, 7.3.4	L1: 35.02, 36.04, 39.01, 49.10 L2: 39.01, 49.02, 49.13, 49.16 L3: 35.03, 49.02, 49.16 L4: 36.05, 36.06, 40.01, 49.01, 49.02, 49.09 L5: 38.01, 49.02, 49.04, 49.09, 49.16 RE: 39.01, 49.02, 49.13, 49.16	Most SCANS are incorporated into this unit, with an emphasis on: • Creative thinking • Interpreting and communicating information • Reasoning	Most EFFs are incorporated into this unit, with an emphasis on: • Conveying ideas in writing • Reading with understanding • Solving problems and making decisions

Listening & Speaking	CASAS Life Skills Competencies	Standardized Student Syllabi/ LCPs	SCANS Competencies	EFF Content Standards
• Talk about banking services and managing money • Discuss budgeting • Talk about ways to save money • Listen to a conversation about ways to save money **Grammar listening:** • Listen to a negotiation conversation **Pronunciation:** • Pauses with commas	**L1:** 0.1.2, 0.1.5, 1.4.6, 1.5.1, 1.5.2, 4.8.1, 7.4.5 **L2:** 0.1.2, 0.1.5, 7.2.2, 7.2.4, 7.2.5 **L3:** 0.1.2, 0.1.5, 0.2.1, 7.2.2, 7.2.5, 7.2.6 **L4:** 0.1.2, 0.1.5, 1.5.1, 6.0.3, 6.0.4, 6.1.1, 6.1.2, 7.4.7 **L5:** 0.1.2, 0.1.5, 0.2.1, 1.1.5, 7.4.4 **RE:** 0.1.2, 0.1.5, 0.2.1, 1.5.1, 7.3.1, 7.3.2, 7.3.4, 7.4.7	**L1:** 49.02, 49.10 **L2:** 49.02, 49.03, 49.13, 49.16 **L3:** 39.01, 49.01, 49.02, 49.09, 49.13, 49.16 **L4:** 49.02, 49.09, 49.16, 49.17 **L5:** 39.01, 49.02, 49.06, 49.09, 49.16 **RE:** 39.01, 49.01, 49.02, 49.16, 49.17	Most SCANS are incorporated into this unit, with an emphasis on: • Acquiring and evaluating information • Interpreting and communicating information • Writing	Most EFFs are incorporated into this unit, with an emphasis on: • Conveying ideas in writing • Cooperating with others • Solving problems and making decisions
• Talk about different types of shopping • Discuss problems experienced when purchasing merchandise • Listen to conversations about a catalog • Listen to a conversation about a problem with a purchase • Discuss consumer rights **Grammar listening:** • Listen for information using participial adjectives **Pronunciation:** • Linked consonants and vowels	**L1:** 0.1.2, 0.1.5, 0.2.1, 1.3.1, 7.2.3, 7.4.5 **L2:** 0.1.2, 0.1.5, 0.2.1, 1.3.3, 1.6.3, 7.4.4 **L3:** 0.1.2, 0.1.5, 7.4.7 **L4:** 0.1.2, 0.1.5, 1.3.3, 1.3.4, 6.0.3, 6.0.4, 6.2.1, 6.2.3, 6.2.5, 7.2.5 **L5:** 0.1.2, 0.1.5, 0.2.1, 1.6.2, 1.6.3, 7.4.2, 7.4.4 **RE:** 0.1.2, 0.1.5, 0.2.1, 4.8.1, 7.2.6, 7.3.1, 7.3.2, 7.3.4	**L1:** 39.01, 45.01, 49.02, 49.10 **L2:** 38.01, 39.01, 45.06, 49.01, 49.02, 49.13, 49.16 **L3:** 49.09, 49.16, 49.17, 50.04, 50.05 **L4:** 49.02, 49.09, 49.16, 51.05 **L5:** 38.01, 39.01, 49.02, 49.04, 49.09, 49.16 **RE:** 39.01, 49.01, 49.02, 49.09, 49.13, 49.16	Most SCANS are incorported into this unit, with an emphasis on: • Arithmetic/Mathematics • Creative thinking • Seeing things in the mind's eye	Most EFFs are incorported into this unit, with an emphasis on: • Conveying ideas in writing • Reflecting and evaluating • Solving problems and making decisions
• Talk about ways to stay healthy • Listen to people's health goals and doctors' advice • Listen to a conversation at a doctor's office • Talk about health insurance issues **Grammar listening:** • Listen to speakers give advice and strong advice **Pronunciation:** • "s" and "ch" sounds	**L1:** 0.1.2, 0.1.5, 3.5.9, 4.8.1 **L2:** 0.1.2, 0.1.5, 0.2.1, 3.5.9 **L3:** 0.1.2, 0.1.5, 0.2.1, 3.5.9, 7.4.7 **L4:** 0.1.2, 0.1.5, 0.2.1, 3.1.3, 3.5.9, 6.0.3, 6.0.4, 6.1.1, 7.5.6 **L5:** 0.1.2, 0.1.5, 2.5.6, 3.2.3, 3.5.9, 7.4.4 **RE:** 0.1.2, 0.1.5, 3.5.9, 4.8.1, 7.2.6, 7.3.1, 7.3.4	**L1:** 41.06, 49.02, 49.10 **L2:** 39.01, 41.06, 49.01, 49.13, 49.16 **L3:** 39.01, 41.06, 49.01, 49.02, 49.09, 49.17 **L4:** 39.01, 41.03, 41.06, 49.02, 49.09, 49.16, 49.17 **L5:** 38.01, 49.02, 49.06, 49.09, 49.16, 50.02 **RE:** 41.06 49.01, 49.02, 49.03, 49.16, 49.17	Most SCANS are incorporated into this unit, with an emphasis on: • Acquiring and evaluating information • Advocating and influencing • Applying technology to the task • Advocating and influencing	Most EFFs are incorporated into this unit, with an emphasis on: • Conveying ideas in writing • Reading with understanding • Solving problems and making decisions

Unit	Life Skills & Civics Competencies	Vocabulary	Grammar	Critical Thinking & Math Concepts	Reading & Writing
Unit 10 **Get Involved!** **page 130**	• Identify community services • Express concern about a community issue • Call a community official for information about an issue or event • Identify ways to get involved in a community • Address community problems • Recognize environmental issues in a community	• Community involvement • Community services • Recycling and dumping terms **In other words:** • Showing understanding **Idiom note:** • *put in (my) two cents*	• Indirect information questions • Indirect questions with *if* and *whether* • Statements with *wh-* and *if/whether* phrases • The suffix *-ment*	• Analyze a community services directory • Speculate on ways to get involved in a community • Analyze an editorial cartoon • Interpret a newspaper editorial on recycling, dumping and related issues **Real-life math:** • Analyze a pie chart **Problem solving:** • Find ways to help with community problems	• Read and write about a community issue • Read a notice of public hearings • Read a newspaper article on community involvement **Writer's note:** • Special purposes of paragraphs in a letter
Unit 11 **Find It on the Net** **page 144**	• Identify Internet and website information • Recognize changes in use of technology • Ask for and clarify instructions about Internet use • Ask and answer questions about partner's life • Offer and respond to help • Identify renters' rights	• The Internet • Website terms **In other words:** • Offering help **Idiom notes:** • *when it comes to* • *it's about time*	• Tag questions and short answers with *be* • Tag questions and short answers with *do* • Question words for clarification	• Analyze a website menu • Compare and contrast technological changes in the past ten years • Speculate about ways to find new homes • Interpret a web article on renters' rights • Speculate about ways the Internet can help renters and home buyers **Real-life math:** • Calculate daily number of hits on a website **Problem solving:** • Learn to work with family members	• Read about changes in the use of technology • Write about using technology • Read an article about renters' rights **Writer's note:** • Using time expressions
Unit 12 **How did I do?** **page 158**	• Identify leadership qualities • Identify personal goals and plans • Ask and answer questions about talents and future plans • Respond to positive and negative feedback • Participate in a performance review • Make polite suggestions and requests	• Achievement terms • Leadership qualities **In other words:** • Responding to feedback **Idiom note:** • *deal with*	• Gerunds after prepositions • Gerunds after *be* + adjective + preposition • Polite requests and suggestions with gerunds • Compound adjectives	• Reflect on personal leadership qualities • Interpret evaluations • Sequence events from an article • Compare and contrast life in the present to life in the past **Real-life math:** • Survey the class, calculate percentages for each answer, and make a pie chart **Problem solving:** • Find ways to help a community	• Read an application essay • Write an application statement • Read an article about a personal achievement **Writer's note:** • Using topic sentences

Listening & Speaking	CASAS Life Skills Competencies	Standardized Student Syllabi/ LCPs	SCANS Competencies	EFF Content Standards
• Discuss community services and involvement • Talk about ways to improve a community • Talk about community meetings and pubic hearings • Listen to directions to city hall • Discuss community problems **Grammar listening:** • Listen for sentences with the same meaning **Pronunciation:** • Pauses in long sentences	**L1:** 0.1.2, 0.1.5, 0.2.1, 5.6.1, 7.4.5 **L2:** 0.1.2, 0.1.5, 0.2.1, 0.2.3, 5.6.1, 5.6.2 **L3:** 5.6.2, 7.5.6 **L4:**0.1.2, 0.1.5, 1.1.3, 5.6.1, 6.0.3, 6.0.4, 6.1.2, 6.7.4, 7.4.7, 7.5.6 **L5:** 0.1.2, 0.1.5, 2.5.6, 5.6.1, 5.7.1, 7.4.4 **RE:** 0.1.2, 0.1.5, 4.8.1, 5.6.1, 5.7.1, 7.2.6, 7.3.1, 7.3.2, 7.3.4	**L1:** 39.01, 49.02, 49.09, 49.10 **L2:** 39.01, 49.01, 49.03, 49.13, 49.16 **L3:** 49.01, 49.02, 49.09, 49.17 **L4:** 49.01, 49.09, 49.16, 49.17, 51.01 **L5:** 38.01, 47.03, 49.02, 49.06, 49.16 **RE:** 47.03, 49.01, 49.02, 49.13, 49.16, 49.17	Most SCANS are incorporated into this unit, with an emphasis on: • Arithmetic/Mathematics • Creative thinking • Seeing things in the mind's eye	Most EFFs are incorporated into this unit, with an emphasis on: • Cooperating with others • Learning through research • Taking responsibility for learning
• Listen to and talk about ways to use computers and the Internet • Talk about ways to find new homes • Listen to an interview about designing a website • Discuss ways landlords and tenants can get along **Grammar listening:** • Listen to questions and complete with the correct tag **Pronunciation:** • Falling and rising intonation of tags	**L1:** 0.1.2, 0.1.5, 0.2.1, 4.8.1, 7.4.4 **L2:** 0.1.2, 0.1.5, 0.2.1, 1.4.1, 4.5.5, 4.5.6, 7.4.4, 7.4.7 **L3:**0.1.2, 0.1.5, 0.1.6, 0.2.1, 7.4.7, 7.5.6 **L4:** 0.1.2, 0.1.5, 0.1.6, 6.0.3, 6.0.4, 6.1.2, 7.5.6 **L5:** 0.1.2, 0.1.5, 1.4.1, 1.4.2, 1.4.3, 1.4.5, 2.5.6, 7.4.4, 7.4.7 **RE:** 0.1.2, 0.1.5, 0.1.6, 0.2.1, 4.8.1, 7.2.6, 7.3.1, 7.3.2, 7.3.4, 7.4.7	**L1:** 38.01, 39.01, 49.02, 49.10 **L2:** 38.01, 39.01, 49.13, 49.16, 49.17 **L3:** 39.01, 49.01, 49.09, 49.13, 49.17 **L4:**49.02, 49.09, 51.05 **L5:** 38.01, 45.01, 45.07, 49.06 **RE:** 39.01, 49.02, 49.13, 49.17	Most SCANS are incorporated into this unit, with an emphasis on: • Creative thinking • Interpreting and communicating information • Listening	Most EFFs are incorporated into this unit, with an emphasis on: • Conveying ideas in writing • Listening actively • Reflecting and evaluating
• Talk about life achievements • Discuss leadership qualities • Listen to conversations between employees and their supervisors • Talk about ways employers can give positive and negative feedback **Grammar listening:** • Listen for sentences with the same meaning **Pronunciation:** • Word grouping in long sentences	**L1:** 0.1.2, 0.1.5, 0.2.1, 4.8.1, 7.4.5 **L2:** 0.1.2, 0.1.5, 0.2.1, 7.1.1 **L3:** 0.1.2, 0.1.5, 0.2.1, 0.2.4, 7.4.7 **L4:** 0.1.2, 0.1.5, 4.4.4, 6.0.3, 6.0.4, 6.2.3, 6.4.2, 6.4.3, 6.7.4, 7.5.6 **L5:**0.1.2, 0.1.5, 2.5.6, 7.2.2, 7.4.4 **RE:** 0.1.2, 0.1.5, 0.2.1, 4.8.1, 7.1.1, 7.2.6, 7.3.1, 7.3.2, 7.3.4, 7.5.6	**L1:** 39.01, 49.02, 49.10 **L2:** 39.01, 49.13, 49.16 **L3:** 39.01, 49.03, 49.09, 49.13, 49.17, 50.06 **L4:** 49.02, 49.09, 49.16, 51.05 **L5:** 38.01, 49.06 **RE:** 39.01, 49.02, 49.13, 49.16	Most SCANS are incorporated into this unit, with an emphasis on: • Knowing how to learn • Participating as a member of a team • Seeing in the mind's eye	Most EFFs are incorporated into this unit, with an emphasis on: • Observing critically • Reading with understanding • Using math to solve problems and communicate

A Word or Two About Reading Introductions to Textbooks

Teaching professionals rarely read a book's introduction. Instead, we flip through the book's pages, using the pictures, topics, and exercises to determine whether the book matches our learners' needs and our teaching style. We scan the reading passages, conversations, writing tasks, and grammar charts to judge the authenticity and accuracy of the text. At a glance, we assess how easy it would be to manage the pair work, group activities, evaluations, and application tasks.

This Introduction, however, also offers valuable information for the teacher. Because you've read this far, I encourage you to read a little further to learn how *Step Forward's* key concepts, components, and multilevel applications will help you help your learners.

Step Forward's Key Concepts

Step Forward is...

- the instructional backbone for single-level and multilevel classrooms.
- a standards-based, performance-based, and topic-based series for low-beginning through high-intermediate learners.
- a source for ready-made, four-skill lesson plans that address the skills our learners need in their workplace, civic, personal, and academic lives.
- a collection of learner-centered, communicative English-language practice activities.

The classroom is a remarkable place. *Step Forward* respects the depth of experience and knowledge that learners bring to the learning process. At the same time, *Step Forward* recognizes that learners' varied proficiencies, goals, interests, and educational backgrounds create instructional challenges for teachers.

To ensure that our learners leave each class having made progress toward their language and life goals, *Step Forward* works from these key concepts:

- **The wide spectrum of learners' needs makes using materials that support multilevel instruction essential.** *Step Forward* works with single-level and multilevel classes.
- **Learners' prior knowledge is a valuable teaching tool.** Prior knowledge questions appear in every *Step Forward* lesson.

- **Learning objectives are the cornerstone of instruction.** Each *Step Forward* lesson focuses on an objective that derives from identified learner needs, correlates to state and federal standards, and connects to a meaningful communication task. Progress toward the objective is evaluated at the end of the lesson.
- **Vocabulary, grammar, and pronunciation skills play an essential role in language learning. They provide learners with the tools needed to achieve life skill, civics, workplace, and academic competencies.** *Step Forward* includes strong vocabulary and grammar strands and features pronunciation and math lesson extensions in each unit.
- **Effective instruction requires a variety of instructional techniques and strategies to engage learners.** Techniques such as Early Production Questioning, Focused Listening, Total Physical Response (TPR), Cooperative Learning, and Problem Solving are embedded in the *Step Forward* series, along with grouping and classroom management strategies.

The *Step Forward* Program

The *Step Forward* program has five levels:

- Intro: pre-beginning
- Book 1: low-beginning
- Book 2: high-beginning
- Book 3: low-intermediate
- Book 4: intermediate to high-intermediate

Each level of *Step Forward* correlates to *The Oxford Picture Dictionary*. For pre-literacy learners, *The Basic Oxford Picture Dictionary Literacy Program* provides a flexible, needs-based approach to literacy instruction. Once learners develop strong literacy skills, they will be able to transition seamlessly into *Step Forward Student Introductory Level*.

Each *Step Forward* level includes the following components:

Step Forward Student Book

A collection of clear, engaging, four-skill lessons based on meaningful learning objectives.

Step Forward Audio Program

The recorded vocabulary, focused listening, conversations, pronunciation, and reading materials from the *Step Forward Student Book*.

Step Forward Step-By-Step Lesson Plans with Multilevel Grammar Exercises CD-ROM

An instructional planning resource with interleaved *Step Forward Student Book* pages, detailed lesson plans featuring multilevel teaching strategies and teaching tips, and a CD-ROM of printable multilevel grammar practice for the structures presented in the *Step Forward Student Book*.

Step Forward Workbook

Practice exercises for independent work in the classroom or as homework.

Step Forward Multilevel Activity Book

More than 100 photocopiable communicative practice activities and 72 picture cards; lesson materials that work equally well in single-level or multilevel settings.

Step Forward Test Generator CD-ROM with ExamView® Assessment Suite

Hundreds of multiple choice and life-skill oriented test items for each *Step Forward Student Book*.

Multilevel Applications of Step Forward

All the *Step Forward* program components support multilevel instruction.

Step Forward is so named because it helps learners "step forward" toward their language and life goals, no matter where they start. Our learners often start from very different places and language abilities within the same class.

Regardless of level, all learners need materials that bolster comprehension while providing an appropriate amount of challenge. This makes multilevel materials an instructional necessity in most classrooms.

Each *Step Forward* lesson provides the following multilevel elements:

- **a general topic or competency area** that works across levels. This supports the concept that members of the class community need to feel connected, despite their differing abilities.
- **clear, colorful visuals and realia** that provide pre-level and on-level support during introduction, presentation and practice exercises, as well as prompts for higher-level questions and exercises.

In addition, *Step Forward* correlates to *The Oxford Picture Dictionary* so that teachers can use the visuals and vocabulary from *The Oxford Picture Dictionary* to support and expand upon each lesson.

- **learner-centered practice exercises** that can be used with same-level or mixed-level pairs or small groups. *Step Forward* exercises are broken down to their simplest steps. Once the exercise has been modeled, learners can usually conduct the exercises themselves.
- **pre-level, on-level, and higher-level objectives for each lesson and the multilevel strategies** necessary to carry out the lesson. These objectives are featured in the *Step-By-Step Lesson Plans*.
- **Grammar Boost pages in the Step Forward Workbook that provide excellent "wait time" activities** for learners who complete an exercise early, thus solving a real issue in the multilevel class.
- **a variety of pair, whole class, and small group activities** in the *Step Forward Multilevel Activity Book*. These activities are perfect for same-level and mixed-level grouping.
- **customizable grammar and evaluation exercises** in the *Step Forward Test Generator CD-ROM with ExamView® Assessment Suite*. These exercises make it possible to create evaluations specific to each level in the class.

Professional Development

As instructors, we need to reflect on second language acquisition in order to build a repertoire of effective instructional strategies. The *Step Forward Professional Development Program* provides research-based teaching strategies, tasks, and activities for single- and multilevel classes.

About Writing an ESL Series

It's collaborative! *Step Forward* is the product of dialogs with hundreds of teachers and learners. The dynamic quality of language instruction makes it important to keep this dialog alive. As you use this book in your classes, I invite you to contact me or any member of the *Step Forward* authorial team with your questions or comments.

Jayme Adelson-Goldstein, Series Director
Stepforwardteam.us@oup.com

Step Forward: All you need to ensure your learners' success.
All the *Step Forward Student Books* follow this format.

LESSON 1: VOCABULARY teaches key words and phrases relevant to the unit topic, and provides conversation practice using the target vocabulary.

New vocabulary is introduced through vibrant art and high-interest listening texts.

Standards-based objectives are identified at the beginning of every lesson.

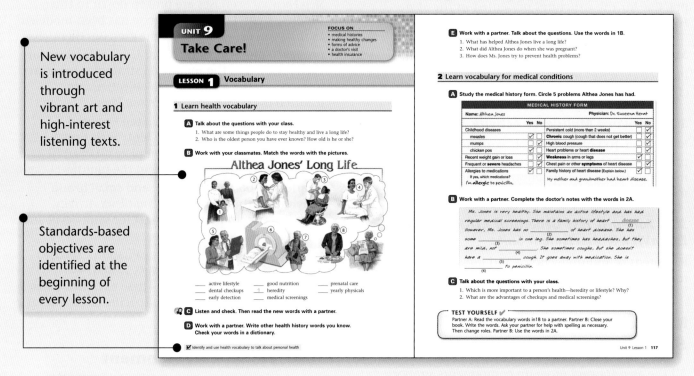

LESSON 2: REAL-LIFE WRITING expands on vocabulary learned in Lesson 1 and furthers learners' understanding through reading and writing about a life skills topic.

Learners write about their personal experiences using the vocabulary.

Life skills readings help learners practice the vocabulary in natural contexts.

LESSON 3: GRAMMAR provides clear, simple presentation of the target structure followed by thorough, meaningful practice of it.

Clear grammar charts make learning grammar easy.

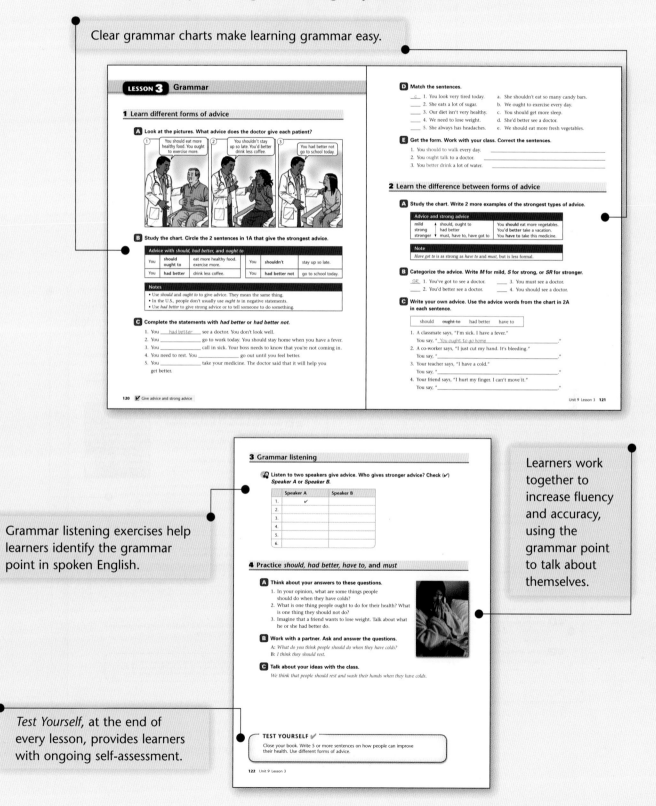

Grammar listening exercises help learners identify the grammar point in spoken English.

Learners work together to increase fluency and accuracy, using the grammar point to talk about themselves.

Test Yourself, at the end of every lesson, provides learners with ongoing self-assessment.

LESSON 4: EVERYDAY CONVERSATION provides learners with fluent, authentic conversations to increase familiarity with natural English.

Model dialogs feature authentic examples of everyday conversation.

Pronunciation activities focus on common areas of difficulty.

Listening activities build listening skills.

Real-life math exercises help learners practice language and math skills.

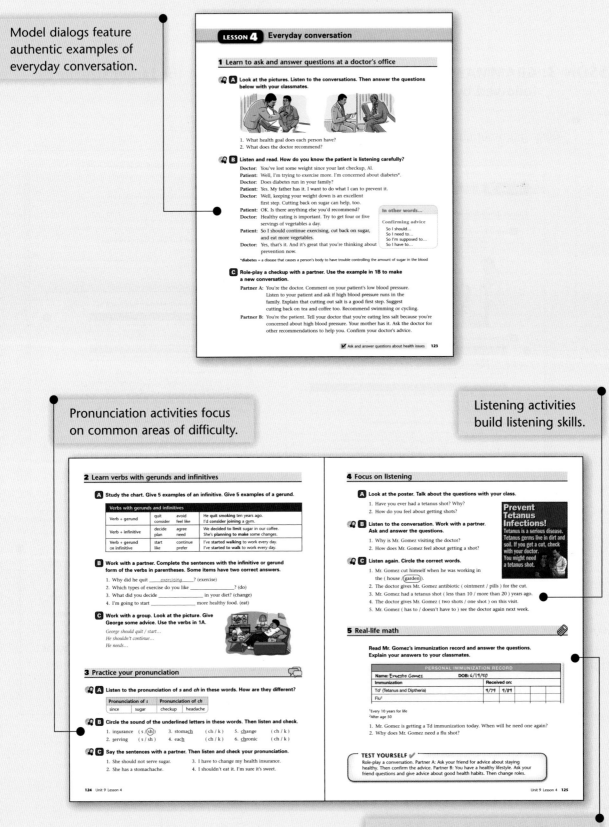

LESSON 5: REAL-LIFE READING develops essential reading skills and offers both life skill and pre-academic reading materials.

High-interest readings recycle vocabulary and grammar.

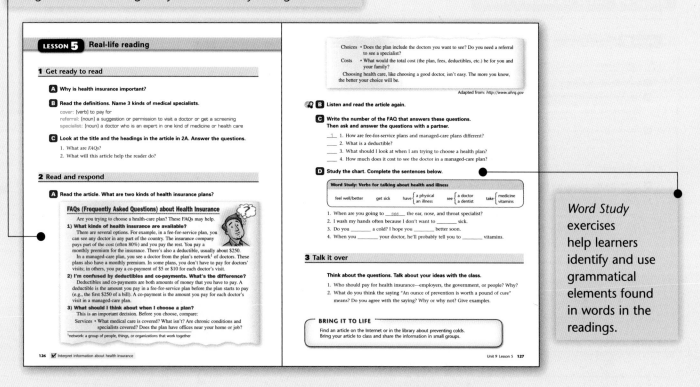

Word Study exercises help learners identify and use grammatical elements found in words in the readings.

REVIEW AND EXPAND includes additional grammar practice and communicative group tasks to ensure your learners' progress.

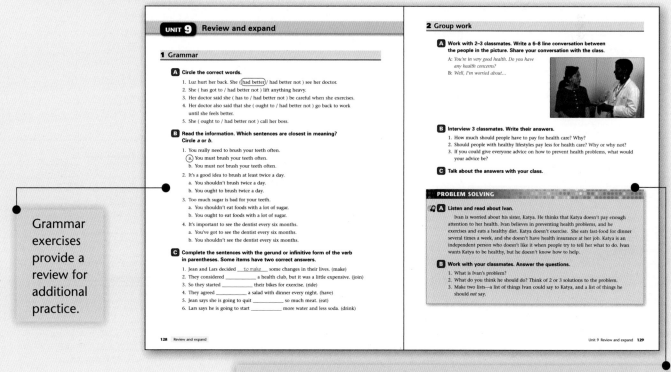

Grammar exercises provide a review for additional practice.

Problem solving tasks encourage learners to use critical thinking skills and meaningful discussion to find solutions to common problems.

Step Forward offers many different components.

Step-By-Step Lesson Plans

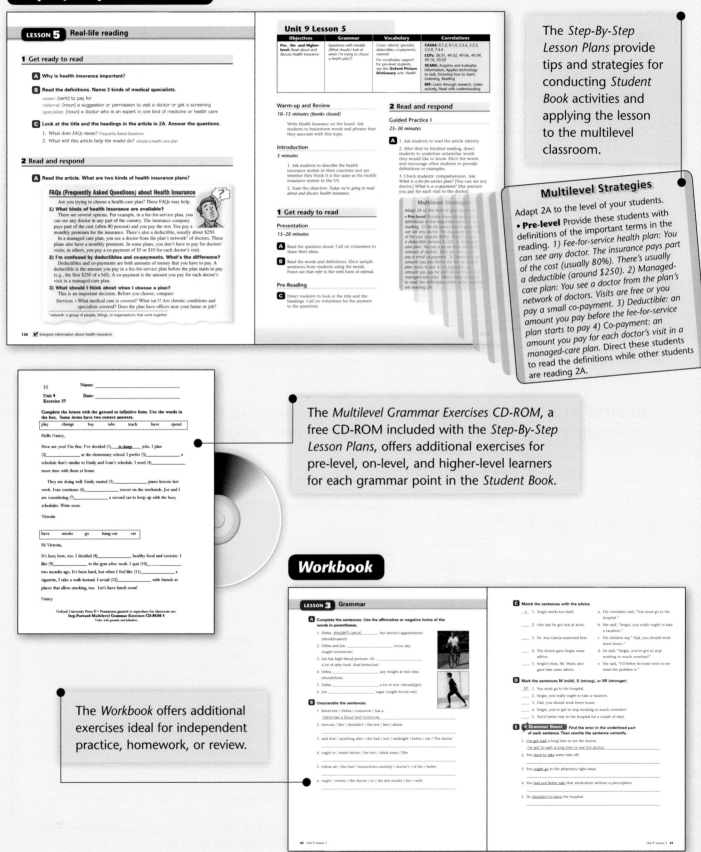

The *Step-By-Step Lesson Plans* provide tips and strategies for conducting *Student Book* activities and applying the lesson to the multilevel classroom.

Multilevel Strategies

Adapt 2A to the level of your students.

• **Pre-level** Provide these students with definitions of the important terms in the reading. 1) *Fee-for-service health plan: You can see any doctor. The insurance pays part of the cost (usually 80%). There's usually a deductible (around $250).* 2) *Managed-care plan: You see a doctor from the plan's network of doctors. Visits are free or you pay a small co-payment.* 3) *Deductible: an amount you pay before the fee-for-service plan starts to pay* 4) *Co-payment: an amount you pay for each doctor's visit in a managed-care plan.* Direct these students to read the definitions while other students are reading 2A.

The *Multilevel Grammar Exercises CD-ROM*, a free CD-ROM included with the *Step-By-Step Lesson Plans*, offers additional exercises for pre-level, on-level, and higher-level learners for each grammar point in the *Student Book*.

Workbook

The *Workbook* offers additional exercises ideal for independent practice, homework, or review.

Multilevel Activity Book

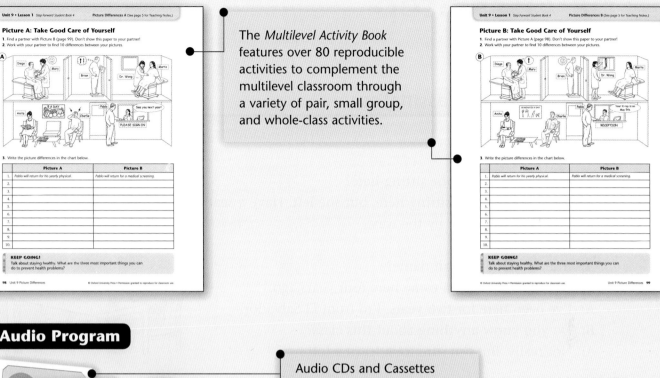

The *Multilevel Activity Book* features over 80 reproducible activities to complement the multilevel classroom through a variety of pair, small group, and whole-class activities.

Audio Program

Audio CDs and Cassettes feature the listening exercises from the *Student Book* as well as conversations, pronunciation, and readings.

Test Generator

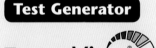
Assessment Suite

The *Test Generator CD-ROM with ExamView® Assessment Suite* offers hundreds of test items for each *Student Book*. Teachers can print out ready-made tests or create their own tests.

Professional Development

Professional Development Task 8

Imagine you want your learners to practice listening carefully during a group task. One behavior you could demonstrate would be leaning forward. Make a list of at least three other behaviors or expressions that careful listeners use.

The *Professional Development Program* offers instructors research-based teaching strategies and activities for single- and multilevel classes, plus Professional Development Tasks like this one.

The First Step

1 Get to know your classmates

STUDENT AUDIO

A **Listen and repeat.**

A: Excuse me. Is anyone sitting here?

B: No. Someone was sitting here, but she left. Have a seat!

A: Thanks. I'm Estela, by the way.

B: Hi Estela. I'm Ara.

A: Ara? Is that a Persian name?

B: No, it's Armenian. I came here four years ago.

A: I've been here for two years. I'm from El Salvador.

B: Do you know anything about this class?

A: Not really. But I'm sure we'll learn a lot!

B **Practice the conversation with 3 classmates. Use your own information.**

2 Review verb tenses

A **Study the sentences and the time lines. Then complete the charts with the verb tenses from the box.**

Future	Present perfect	Simple past
Past continuous	Present continuous	~~Simple present~~

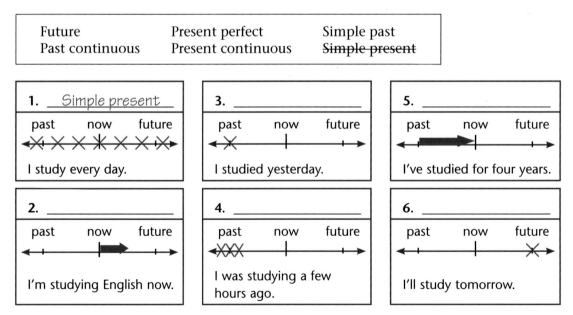

1. _Simple present_

past · now · future

I study every day.

2. _____

past · now · future

I'm studying English now.

3. _____

past · now · future

I studied yesterday.

4. _____

past · now · future

I was studying a few hours ago.

5. _____

past · now · future

I've studied for four years.

6. _____

past · now · future

I'll study tomorrow.

B Work with a partner. Read the questions and identify the tenses. Then ask and answer the questions.

1. What are you thinking about right now?
2. What do you do on weekends?
3. How long have you studied English?
4. What did you do last Saturday?
5. Where will you speak English this week?

3 Word families

A Look at the chart. Then complete the sentences.

Word	Part of speech
study	verb
student	noun

Word	Part of speech
studious	adjective (adj.)
studiously	adverb (adv.)

1. Sara is a part-time _____student_____.
2. She _____ hard every day.
3. She does research every night. She's really _____.
4. She's working _____ because she has a biology exam tomorrow.

B Look in a dictionary to find the word family for the word *help*. Then complete the chart.

Word	Part of speech	Example
help	noun	This dictionary is a big ___help___. I like it a lot.
	verb	I think this class will really _____ me.
	adj.	Our teacher is friendly and very _____.
	adv.	Ara _____ gave me his pencil.

C Work with a partner. Look in the dictionary for another word family. Then complete the chart.

Word	Part of speech	Example

D Talk about your word family with the class.

UNIT 1

It Takes All Kinds!

FOCUS ON
- personalities and learning styles
- describing yourself
- action and non-action verbs
- expressing opinions about education
- test anxiety

LESSON 1 Vocabulary

1 Learn personality and talent vocabulary

A Talk about the questions with your class.

1. Which are you best at—math, languages, or sports?
2. Do you like to draw? Why or why not?

B Work with your classmates. Match the words with the pictures.

| ____ adventurous | ____ athletic | ____ musical | ____ social |
| ____ artistic | ____ mathematical | ____ quiet | _1_ verbal |

C Listen and check. Then read the new words with a partner.

D Work with a partner. Write other personality and talent words you know. Check your words in a dictionary.

☑ Identify personality traits, talents, and learning styles

E Work with a partner. Practice the conversation. Use the words in 1B.

A: What kind of person are you?

B: I'm pretty athletic. How about you?

A: Well, I'm not very athletic, but I'm artistic.

2 Learn vocabulary for learning styles

A Read the article. Who are you more like—Ria, Tony, or Trang?

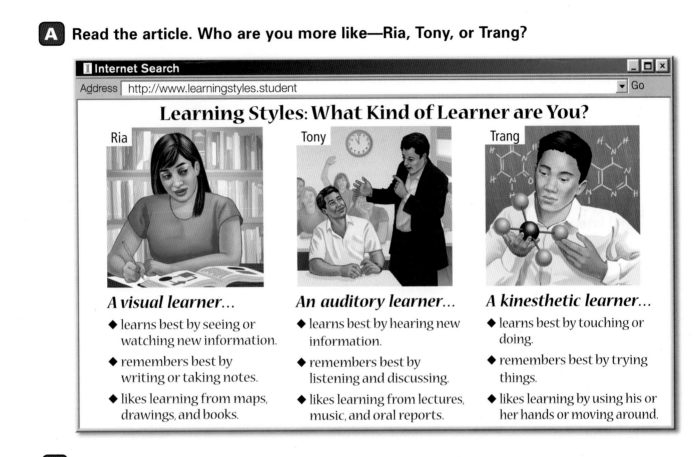

Internet Search

Address http://www.learningstyles.student ▾ Go

Learning Styles: What Kind of Learner are You?

Ria

Tony

Trang

A *visual learner*...

◆ learns best by seeing or watching new information.

◆ remembers best by writing or taking notes.

◆ likes learning from maps, drawings, and books.

An *auditory learner*...

◆ learns best by hearing new information.

◆ remembers best by listening and discussing.

◆ likes learning from lectures, music, and oral reports.

A *kinesthetic learner*...

◆ learns best by touching or doing.

◆ remembers best by trying things.

◆ likes learning by using his or her hands or moving around.

B Work with a partner. Match the names with the actions.

When there is a problem with the computer,

_____ 1. Ria   a. asks someone to tell him how to fix it.

_____ 2. Tony   b. tries to fix the problem.

_____ 3. Trang   c. reads the instruction book.

C Talk about the questions with your class.

1. Which words in this lesson describe you? Which describe your friends and classmates?
2. How many visual, auditory, and kinesthetic learners are there in your class?

TEST YOURSELF ✔

Close your book. Work with a partner. Make a list of as many new words from the lesson as you can. Alphabetize your list. Then check your spelling in a dictionary.

1 Read about learning styles

A Look at the pictures. Talk about the questions with your class.

1. Name something you have recently learned to do. How did you learn to do it?
2. How do you like to learn new information? From a teacher? From books? Why?

B Listen and read the paragraph.

My Learning Style

by Carlos Morales

I think I'm an auditory learner. When I have to learn something new, I like to hear about it first. For example, at work I remember things if my boss tells me about them, but I often forget information if I read it in a memo. At home, I don't spend much time reading newspapers or magazines. I prefer to listen to the news on TV or on the radio. When I'm cooking or doing housework, I like to listen to interviews on radio talk shows. I learn a lot from them! In class, I understand best when I hear new information from the teacher. I don't learn very well from sources like books or websites. I'm really social and I like studying and learning with other people.

Writer's note

You can introduce an example with *For example* and a comma (,).

C Check your understanding. Mark the sentences T (true), F (false), or NI (no information).

__F__ 1. The writer likes to learn new information by reading.

____ 2. He'd rather listen to TV and radio news than read the newspaper.

____ 3. When he's cleaning or cooking, he watches TV.

____ 4. When he studies at home, he turns the radio on.

____ 5. In the classroom, he learns by listening to his teacher.

☑ Write a paragraph to describe one's learning style

2 Write about your learning style

 A **Talk about the questions with your class.**

1. How are you similar to the writer in 1B?
2. How are you different from the writer in 1B?

B **Write a paragraph about your learning style. Use the model in 1B and the questions below to help you.**

- What kind of learner do you think you are?
- How do you remember new information?
- What do you do at home to learn new information?
- How do you learn best in class?
- Which do you prefer—studying and learning alone or with other people?

> My Learning Style
>
> by (your name)
>
> I think I'm a visual learner.
>
> I learn best by seeing new
>
> information...

C **Use the checklist to edit your writing. Check (✔) the true sentences.**

Editing checklist	
1. I described my learning and studying styles.	
2. I included one or more examples.	
3. I introduced one example with *For example* and a comma (,).	
4. Every sentence starts with a capital letter and ends with a period.	

D **Exchange paragraphs with a partner. Read and comment on your partner's work.**

1. Point out one example that you think is interesting.
2. Ask your partner a question about his or her learning style.

TEST YOURSELF ✔

Write a new paragraph. Describe your partner's or another person's learning style.

1 Learn action verbs in the present

A Read the story. Name 3 creative things Antonia does.

Antonia is the most creative person in our class. She works in an office during the day, but on the weekends she paints pictures and writes poems. She doesn't watch TV.

Right now Antonia isn't painting pictures and she isn't writing poems. She's making a blouse. She makes all of her own clothes.

B Study the charts. Circle the 5 simple present action verbs and underline the 3 present continuous action verbs in the story above.

ACTION VERBS IN THE SIMPLE PRESENT AND THE PRESENT CONTINUOUS

Simple present
Antonia often **makes** her own clothes.
She **doesn't watch** TV.
They sometimes **write** poems.
They **don't paint** pictures very often.

Present continuous
She **is making** a blouse.
She **isn't watching** TV now.
They **are writing** poems now.
They **aren't painting** pictures now.

Note
Most verbs describe actions. These verbs are called action verbs.

C Complete the sentences with the simple present or the present continuous form of the verbs in parentheses.

1. Pedro Santana _____works_____ at a university in the math department. (work)

2. In his free time, he _____ math books for school children. (write)

3. Today is Saturday, and Pedro _____ at the university now. (not work)

4. Right now, he and his family _____ their house. (paint)

5. The Santanas _____ much TV on weekends. (not watch)

6. His children _____ their homework now. (not do)

7. Now they _____ Pedro paint. (help)

8. Pedro always _____ his friends, "It's important for families to do things together." (tell)

✔ Use action and non-action verbs to describe the present

2 Learn non-action verbs in the simple present

A Study the charts. Is *be* an action verb or a non-action verb?

NON-ACTION VERBS IN THE SIMPLE PRESENT

Non-action verbs
Ari **likes** books about science and travel.
He **knows** a lot about the outdoors.
Ari **thinks** everyone should spend time outdoors.
He **sees** a lot of different things on his travels.
Ari **has** a website with pictures from his trips.
He **is** a good photographer.

More non-action verbs		
believe	need	smell
dislike	own	sound
forget	possess	taste
hate	remember	understand
hear	seem	want
love		

Notes
• We use non-action (stative) verbs to describe feelings, knowledge, beliefs, and the senses.
• These verbs are usually **not** used in the present continuous:

        He knows a lot.

         * He is knowing a lot. (INCORRECT)

B Work with a partner. Complete the conversation. Use the words in the box.

think	~~remember~~	seem	have	know	don't understand

A: Do you _____remember_____ the page number for
               (1)
    our homework assignment?

B: Yes, it's page 23.

A: Thanks. Hey, these questions _____ really easy.
                                   (2)

B: Great! By the way, does this book _____ an answer key?
                                        (3)

A: I don't _____. OK, let's get started.
               (4)

B: Uh-oh. I _____ question one. Do you?
               (5)

A: No. I don't. I _____ this assignment is going to take all day!
               (6)

C Circle the correct words.

1. I really (**love** / am loving) to study history.
2. I (study / am studying) history every Saturday.
3. I also (like / am liking) to read.
4. Right now I (read / am reading) an interesting book about U.S. history.
5. I (know / am knowing) a lot about history.
6. I (think / am thinking) everyone should learn about the past.

3 Grammar listening

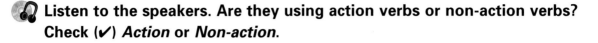 **Listen to the speakers. Are they using action verbs or non-action verbs? Check (✔) *Action* or *Non-action*.**

	Action	Non-action
1.		✔
2.		
3.		
4.		
5.		
6.		

4 Practice action and non-action verbs

A **Think about your answers to these questions.**

1. How do you remember new words?
   Name two different ways.
2. Do you think that English is an easy language?
   Why or why not?
3. How do you feel when you speak English?
4. What do you like about English?
   What do you dislike?
5. What are three things that you often do
   in your English class?
6. Which of these things are you doing today?
7. What are you doing right now that you always do in class?

B **Work with a partner. Ask and answer the questions in 4A.**

A: *How do you remember new words?*
B: *Well, sometimes I repeat the new word. Other times, I use it in a sentence.*

C **Talk about your partner with the class.**

Nancy sometimes repeats a new word. Sometimes she uses it in a sentence.

TEST YOURSELF ✔

Close your book. Write 5 sentences about yourself and 5 about your classmates. Use a simple present or present continuous verb in each sentence. Use at least 3 non-action verbs.

1 Learn to express opinions about education

A Look at the picture. Listen to the conversations. Then answer the questions below with your classmates.

1. Do the man and woman agree on how many students should be in a class? What is the man's opinion? What is the woman's opinion?
2. Do they agree that teaching is hard work? What is the man's opinion? What is the woman's opinion?

B Listen and read. What do the people disagree about?

A: I think watching TV is the best way to learn English.
B: I'm not sure I agree. I think it's better to talk and listen to people.
A: Really? Why do you think so?
B: Because when you talk to people, there's real communication.
A: You have a point, but I still think watching TV is best.

In other words...

Disagreeing politely

I'm not sure I agree.
You have a point, but…
Maybe you're right, but…
That's true, but…

C Role-play a conversation about opinions with a partner. Use the example in 1B to make a new conversation.

Partner A: State your opinion. You think that the best way to talk to a teacher is to use *Mr.* or *Ms.* and the teacher's last name. Listen to your partner's opinion. Explain that you think that using a teacher's first name doesn't sound polite.

Partner B: Disagree politely with your partner. Say that you prefer to call teachers by their first names. Explain that you think this is OK when both students and teachers are adults.

2 Review *Yes/No*, information, and *or* questions

A Study the charts. Then match the questions with the answers.

Yes/No questions and short answers	
A: Do you agree? **B:** Yes, I **do**.	**A: Does** watching TV help you learn? **B:** No, it **doesn't**.

Information questions	
A: Why do you think so? **B:** Because I heard it on the radio.	**A: Who** agrees with you? **B:** Everyone agrees with me!

Or questions	
A: Does he like to learn from books **or** TV? **B:** He likes to learn from books.	**A:** Do they agree **or** disagree? **B:** They agree.

___c___ 1. When do you study?

_____ 2. Do you need a quiet place to study?

_____ 3. Do you like or dislike the Internet?

_____ 4. What does *visual* mean?

_____ 5. How much does this book cost?

   a. Yes, I do.

   b. $12.99.

   c. After my children are asleep.

   d. It means using your eyes.

   e. I like it, but I don't use it often.

B Work with a partner. Ask and answer the questions.

1. What is one thing you remember about school in the past?
2. Do you think learning English is easy? Why or why not?

3 Practice your pronunciation

A Listen to the pronunciation of the *t* sounds in these sentences.

The pronunciation of *t*	
It's better to talk and listen. There's real communication.	The *tt* in *better* is pronounced /d/. The *t* in *talk* is pronounced /t/. The *t* in *listen* is not pronounced. The *t* in *communication* is pronounced /sh/.

B Work with a partner. How do you think the *t* is pronounced in these words? Write *d, t, sh,* or *NP* (not pronounced).

___t___ 1. study   _____ 3. after   _____ 5. little

_____ 2. teacher   _____ 4. education   _____ 6. mortgage

C Listen and check. Then read the words with a partner.

4 Focus on listening

A **Look at the picture. Talk about the questions with your class.**

1. Where are the people?
2. What are they doing?

B **Listen to the conversation. Check (✔) the issues the people talk about.**

| ✔ 1. teachers' salaries | ____ 3. cafeteria food | ____ 5. safety |
| ____ 2. class size | ____ 4. libraries | ____ 6. need for books |

C **Listen again. Do the speakers agree or disagree on the best solutions to the problems? Check (✔) Agree or Disagree.**

	Solutions	Agree	Disagree
1.	Pay teachers more.	✔	
2.	Build new schools.		
3.	Raise taxes.		
4.	Put in security cameras.		
5.	Buy new books and computers.		

5 Real-life math

A **Look at the graph and answer the question.**

What was the average* number of students per class at Hills Adult School for the four-year period from 2003 to 2006? _____

*average = total number of students for 4 years, divided by 4

B **Explain your answer to your classmates.**

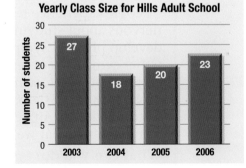

Yearly Class Size for Hills Adult School

TEST YOURSELF ✔

Role-play a conversation about weekend classes. Partner A: You think schools should have some weekend classes. Explain why. Partner B: Disagree politely. You think most students don't like weekend classes. Explain why. Then change roles.

1 Get ready to read

A How do you feel about taking tests?

B Read the definitions. Which word can you use to describe your work?

college entrance exam: (noun) a test students take to get into a college or university

concentrate: (verb) to give all your attention to something

manageable: (adj.) not too big or difficult to control

C Look at the title, the picture, and the section headings in the article in 2A. What do you think the article is about?

2 Read and respond

A Read the article. What is test anxiety?

Internet Search _ □ x

Address `http://www.testanxiety.article` ▼ Go

Test Anxiety: It's Not Just for Students!

How did you feel the last time you took a test? Does a driving test, a test at work, a practice GED exam, or a college entrance exam make you nervous? Tests are a part of life today, and for many people, test anxiety is, too.

What is test anxiety?

People experience test anxiety when they feel extremely nervous about studying for or taking a test. Many people develop physical symptoms such as headaches and nausea. Other symptoms of test anxiety are emotional, such as crying easily and feeling annoyed or frustrated. The major problem with test anxiety, though, is its effect on our ability to think clearly. Anxiety can make it difficult to concentrate or remember what we've learned.

What can you do?

Experts recommend using these strategies[1] to control test anxiety:

- Prepare for tests. Decide on a study schedule and follow it.
- Take good care of yourself. Get enough sleep, eat well, exercise, and give yourself some relaxation time.
- Get to the exam a little early—about 15 minutes.

---

[1]strategies: plans you use to achieve something

☑ Read and reflect on an article about text anxiety

- If you feel very nervous during the exam, take a few deep breaths. Calm down by saying to yourself, "I studied and I'm going to do fine on this test."

Tests are a fact of modern life, and most of us feel some anxiety when we have to take them. The next time you have to take a test, follow the experts' suggestions to bring your anxiety to a manageable level. You'll see: they help!

Adapted from: *www.hsc.edu and www.sdc.uwo.ca*

B Listen and read the article again.

C Circle the correct answer or answers.

1. Someone with test anxiety might feel ____.
   a. annoyed
   b. energetic
   c. nauseous

2. The most serious problem with test anxiety is its effect on our ____.
   a. emotions
   b. health
   c. ability to concentrate

3. If the test begins at 2:00, you should arrive at ____.
   a. 1:00
   b. 1:45
   c. 2:00

4. The experts advise people with test anxiety to ____.
   a. talk to other people taking the test
   b. take deep breaths
   c. calm down

5. Experts say test-taking strategies can help you ____.
   a. manage anxiety
   b. sleep at night
   c. study

3 Talk it over

Think about the questions. Talk about your ideas with the class.

1. Name a test you have taken in the U.S. How did you feel before you took it? After you took it?
2. Some people think that children have to take too many tests in school. Do you agree? Why or why not?

BRING IT TO LIFE

Use the library or the Internet to find a learning-styles test. Take the test and check your results. Bring your test to class. Do you agree with the results? Why or why not? Talk about your ideas with your classmates.

1 Grammar

A Circle the non-action verbs and underline the action verbs.

1. Lucy goes out with her friends every weekend, and she (loves) social events.
2. She has 100 phone numbers in her cell phone, and she calls her friends every week.
3. Her brothers, Steve and Ben, seem less social because they spend a lot of time at home.
4. Ben reads about the stars and planets because he likes astronomy.
5. Steve doesn't talk much, but he remembers everything he reads.

B Complete the conversations. Circle the correct words.

A: Juan ((thinks) / is thinking) that Hills Adult School is a good school.
             (1)

B: I (agree / am agreeing) with him. They (have / are having) good teachers.
        (2)   (3)

A: I've heard that they (start / are starting) some new classes now.
                      (4)

B: That's right. I (go / am going) there right now. (Are you wanting / Do you want) to
                (5)   (6)

   come with me?

C Match the parts of the questions. Then ask your partner the questions.

  _b_ 1. When do we   a. include?

  ____ 2. Do you like morning classes   b. get our books?

  ____ 3. Does the school sell books   c. a lot of homework?

  ____ 4. Do you know   d. or give them to students?

  ____ 5. What does the price of the class   e. or evening classes?

  ____ 6. Does the teacher give   f. everyone's name yet?

D Read the answers. Complete the questions with the simple present.

1. **A:** Why _____does Mitch hate_____ tests?

   B: Mitch hates tests because he often doesn't do well on them.

2. **A:** How _____ before an exam?

   B: He feels nauseous before an exam.

3. **A:** What time _____ when he has an exam?

   B: He gets up at 5 a.m. when he has an exam.

4. **A:** What _____ about test anxiety?

   B: Experts say we can control test anxiety.

2 Group work

 A **Work with 2–3 classmates. Write a 6–8 line conversation between the people in the picture. Share your conversation with the class.**

A: *What's your opinion of this program?*
B: *Well,…*

B **Interview 3 classmates. Write their answers.**

1. What are three words from this unit that describe you?
2. What is one word from this unit that doesn't describe you?
3. Do you think you are mostly a visual, an auditory, or a kinesthetic learner?
4. What is the best way for you to study? Why?
5. In your opinion, what's the best way to control test anxiety?

Fernando

1. artistic, social, visual

C **Talk about the answers with your class.**

PROBLEM SOLVING

 A **Listen and read about Rita.**

Rita lives with two roommates. They're all good friends. Rita works part-time and goes to school. Her roommates aren't students; they work. Rita's classes are challenging, and she often has a lot of homework. She studies best when the apartment is quiet. But when her roommates come home from work, they don't want to be quiet. They want to enjoy the evening. When they talk and play music, Rita can't concentrate. She doesn't know what to do.

B **Work with your classmates. Answer the questions.**

1. What is Rita's problem?
2. What could she do? Think of 2 or 3 solutions to her problem.
3. Write a short letter to Rita. Tell her what you think she should do.

UNIT 2

Keeping Current

FOCUS ON
- getting the news
- writing a news story
- past passives
- talking about the news
- reading a news report

LESSON 1 Vocabulary

1 Learn newspaper vocabulary

A Talk about the questions with your class.

1. How do you get the news?
2. What kind of news is the most important to you?

B Work with your classmates. Match the words with the pictures.

_____ classified ads   _____ entertainment section   _____ lifestyle section

_____ editorial page   _1_ front page   _____ sports section

C Listen and check. Then read the new words with a partner.

D Work with a partner. Write other newspaper words you know.
Check your words in a dictionary.

E Work with a partner. Practice the conversation. Use the words in 1B.

A: Do you read the editorial page every day?

B: Not every day. But I always check the sports section. What about you?

A: I usually just read the front page.

2 Learn more news vocabulary

A Look at the website. What kind of website is this?

Internet Search	_ □ x

Address http://www.newspaper.news ▼ Go

Your source for breaking news and current events, updated 24 hours a day! | Search

Home	**Top Story**		**Current Events**	**Weather Forecast**
Local	**Bus Fares Going up**		Latest news: President will make a speech tonight.	Check your local weather here.
National		To see related articles, click here.		
International				
Health		**Traffic Report**	Senators vote on tax bill.	Today Tomorrow
Technology		Up-to-the-minute traffic information.		

This Hour's Headlines

School Closed After Fire

Business News: New Mall Planned

This Week at the Movies

Special interview with *Please Don't Say Goodbye* co-star, Joni Marie Forester.

| Education |
| Business |

B Work with a partner. Match the news vocabulary with the definitions.

1. _e_ top story
2. ____ traffic report
3. ____ current events
4. ____ weather forecast
5. ____ headlines

a. information about highway conditions
b. information on the state, local and national weather
c. news stories and events that have happened recently
d. the titles of important news stories
e. the most important or most recent news event

C Talk about the questions with your class.

1. Which section of the newspaper is most interesting or important to you?
2 Do you read a newspaper or visit a news website every day? Why or why not?
3. What kind of news do you never read?

TEST YOURSELF ✔

Work with a partner. Partner A: Read the vocabulary words in 1B to your partner. Partner B: Close your book. Write the words. Ask your partner for help with spelling as necessary. Then change roles. Partner B: Use the words in 2B.

1 Read a news story

 A Look at the picture. Talk about the questions with your class.

1. What happened on this street?
2. How do you think the neighbors feel?

STUDENT AUDIO **B** Listen and read the news story.

Police Called in Lakeland

Tues. November 8 A group of teenagers painted graffiti on an empty building in Lakeland last night. Angry neighbors saw them and called the police. The police responded to the call, and the teens were taken to the Lakeland Police Station.

Neighbors disagree about the graffiti. Some people don't like it. They say that it is changing the way the neighborhood looks. However, the building's owner, Mr. Anwar Suk, doesn't mind the graffiti. He says that it is neighborhood art. Next week, the chief of police will hold a community meeting to talk about the neighborhood disagreement.

> **Writer's note**
>
> A news story answers the questions *who, what, when, where,* and *why*.

C Check your understanding. Work with a partner. Ask and answer the questions.

1. What happened? Where did it happen? When did it happen?
2. Why were the teenagers taken to the police station?
3. What is the neighborhood disagreement?
4. What is going to happen next?

2 Write a news story

A Talk about the questions with your class.

1. Name three or four recent local, national, or international events.
2. Choose one event. What happened?

B Write a news story about a recent event in your community, in the nation, or in the world. Use the model in 1B and the questions below to help you.

Paragraph 1: What happened?
When and where did it happen?
Who was involved?
Why did it happen?

Paragraph 2: How did people react to the event?
What do you think is going to happen next?

> Robbery in Lakeland
>
> Two men robbed a bank in Lakeland
>
> yesterday...

C Use the checklist to edit your writing. Check (✔) the true sentences.

Editing checklist	
1. My news story tells about an event that happened recently.	
2. It answers the questions *who, what, when, where,* and *why.*	
3. My story has two paragraphs.	
4. The first line of each paragraph is indented.	

D Exchange stories with a partner. Read and comment on your partner's work.

1. Point out one part of the story that you think is interesting.
2. Ask your partner a question about the current event in his or her news story.

TEST YOURSELF ✔

Write a new news story about another interesting event at your workplace, in your neighborhood, or at your school.

1 Learn the past passive

A Read the article. What caused the accident on Highway 437?

Highway 437 Closed by Multi-Car Accident

by Min Pham

Highway 437 was closed by the police for six hours last night after heavy fog caused a multi-car accident. Paramedics arrived in two ambulances. Several people were taken to the hospital. The highway was closed while the damaged cars were removed from the road. The highway was reopened just before midnight.

B Study the chart. Underline the 4 past passive sentences in the article above.

The past passive		
┌── Subject ──┐	┌── *was/were* + past participle ──┐	
An accident	**was caused**	by the fog last night.
Min	**wasn't taken**	to the hospital by the paramedics.
Several people	**were taken**	to the hospital after the accident.
The cars	**weren't removed**	for two hours because of the fog.

Notes

• We usually use the active voice to say what people or things do.
   The paramedics took the injured people to the hospital.
• We use the passive voice when we don't know who performed the action, when it isn't important who performed the action, or when it's clear who performed the action.
   The injured people were taken to the hospital. (It's clear that they were taken by the paramedics.)

C Complete the sentences with the past passive. Use the verbs in parentheses.

1. The accident ___was caused___ by the heavy fog. (cause)

2. The road _____ by the police. (close)

3. The article _____ after the accident. (write)

4. The pictures _____ by a local news photographer. (take)

☑ Use the past passive to discuss and write about current events

D Get the form. Work with your class. Correct the sentences.

1. The Teller School was close on Thursday because of a fire.

   <u>The Teller School was closed on</u>
   <u>Thursday because of a fire.</u>

2. The fire caused by lightning.

   _____

3. Parents was told to pick up their children.

   _____

4. The school was reopen on Friday.

   _____

E Rewrite the sentences in the past passive. Use *by* + noun to say who performed the action.

1. After the accident, the police closed Highway 437.

   <u>After the accident, Highway 437 was closed by the police.</u>

2. The paramedics took the injured people to the hospital.

   _____

3. The tow trucks removed the cars from the highway.

   _____

4. The police reopened the highway an hour later.

   _____

2 Learn past passive questions

A Study the charts. Which words come first in *Yes/No* questions?

PAST PASSIVE QUESTIONS

Yes/No questions
A: Was the highway **reopened**? **B:** Yes, it was.
A: Were people **taken** to the hospital? **B:** Yes, they were.

Information questions
A: When **was** the highway **reopened**? **B:** It was reopened an hour after the accident.
A: Where **were** the injured people **taken**? **B:** They were taken to City Hospital.

B Complete the conversation with the past passive of the verbs in parentheses.

A: There was a big accident on the highway this morning.

B: Really? What caused the accident?

A: It ___was caused___ by two deer. (cause) They ran across the road.
      (1)

B: _____ anyone _____? (hit)
         (2)   (2)

A: No. Thankfully no one _____. (hit)
                                (3)

B: What about the deer? _____ they _____? (hurt)
                              (4)   (4)

A: One deer _____ (hit). It _____. (not hurt)
                  (5)   (6)

3 Grammar listening

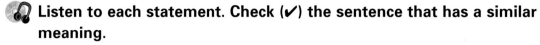

🎧 **Listen to each statement. Check (✔) the sentence that has a similar meaning.**

1. _____ a.   Our car hit a tree.
   ✔ b.   A tree hit our car.
2. _____ a.   The neighbors gave the information to the reporter.
   _____ b.   The reporter gave the information to the neighbors.
3. _____ a.   The teenagers' parents called the police.
   _____ b.   The police called the teenagers' parents.
4. _____ a.   A fire caused an electrical problem.
   _____ b.   An electrical problem caused the fire.

4 Practice the past passive

A **Think of 3 news stories you have heard in the last few months. Answer as many of the questions as you can.**

1. What was built? Where? Why? When?
2. Who was rescued?
3. What was closed?
4. What was damaged?
5. Who was robbed? What was stolen?

B **Work with a partner. Talk about the news stories that you thought of. Use the past passive.**

A: *A few weeks ago a woman was rescued in the mountains.*
B: *Really? Who rescued her?*
A: *I think she was rescued by the park service.*

C **Talk about the news stories with the class.**

A woman was rescued in the mountains.

TEST YOURSELF ✔

Close your book. Write 5 sentences about your classmates' news stories. Use the past passive.

1 Learn to talk about a current event

STUDENT
AUDIO

A Look at the picture. Listen to the conversation. Then answer the questions below with your classmates.

1. What did the city want to do?
2. Why did the protesters disagree with the city?

STUDENT
AUDIO

B Listen and read. What did the protesters want?

A: Did you hear about the protest yesterday?

B: No. What was it about?

A: The city wanted to cut down a hundred-year-old tree in the park, and protesters tied themselves to the tree.

B: A hundred trees?

A: No, not a hundred trees, a *hundred-year-old* tree. The protesters were very upset.

B: I can understand that. We have to protect the environment. So was the tree cut down?

A: No. To make a long story short,* the protesters won. The tree was saved.

*****Idiom note:** to make a long story short = to tell the most important fact

> **In other words...**
>
> **Expressing agreement**
> I can understand that.
> That makes sense to me.
> I'd agree with that.

C Role-play a conversation about a current event with a partner. Use the example in 1B to make a new conversation.

Partner A: Tell your friend about a story on the news: there was a protest at the high school because the school board wanted to prohibit cell phones in school. The students were upset and protested at lunch. The students won. Cell phones weren't prohibited.

Partner B: At first, you don't understand your friend. You think the school wanted to sell phones to students. You understand the students. Cell phones are important in an emergency. Ask if cell phones were prohibited.

2 Learn reflexive pronouns

A Study the charts. How do reflexive pronouns end?

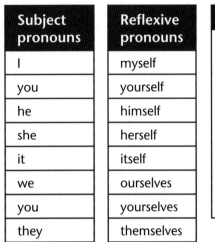

Subject pronouns	Reflexive pronouns
I	myself
you	yourself
he	himself
she	herself
it	itself
we	ourselves
you	yourselves
they	themselves

Notes

- Reflexive pronouns end with *-self* or *-selves*.
- They are used when the subject and object of the sentence refer to the same people or things.
  I hurt **myself**.
- Use *by* + reflexive pronoun to say that someone or something is alone or does something without help.
  She went **by herself**. = She went alone.

B Work with a partner. Complete the sentences with reflexive pronouns.

1. Did you see the protest ___yourself___, or did you hear about it on the news?
2. We were watching the news, and we saw _____ on TV!
3. Did you and Paul go by _____, or did Tim go with you?
4. He was surprised to see a picture of _____ in the newspaper.

C Work with a partner. Ask and answer the question.

What are some things you like to do by yourself?

3 Practice your pronunciation

STUDENT
AUDIO

A Listen to the conversation. Notice how the speakers use stress to clarify their meaning.

A: The city wanted to cut down a hundred-year-old tree.
B: A hundred trees?
A: No, not a hundred trees, *a hundred-year-old* tree.

B Work with a partner. Underline the words you think are stressed.

1. A: The tree wasn't cut down.
   B: It was cut down?
   A: No, it wasn't cut down.

2. A: The protesters were very upset.
   B: The police were upset?
   A: No, the protesters.

STUDENT
AUDIO

C Listen and check. Then practice the conversations in 3A and 3B with a partner.

4 Focus on listening

A **Talk about the questions with your class.**

1. How often do you listen to news on the radio?

2. When is reporting the news a dangerous job? Give examples.

B **Listen to the news story. Answer the questions.**

1. Where is the news reporter?

2. What weather condition is causing problems?

C **Listen again. Circle the correct words.**

1. People think that the hurricane will arrive (today / (Wednesday)).

2. Timothy is the name of the (reporter / hurricane).

3. People have to leave their homes (today / tomorrow).

4. People will be able to stay in (schools / hotels) during the hurricane.

5. Local officials asked news reporters to (stay / leave).

6. Ron Avery is a reporter for (Channel 4 / Channel 5) News.

5 Real-life math

A **Read the story and answer the question.**

Before the hurricane hit, 100,000 Floridians left their homes. Luckily, when the hurricane hit, very few homes were damaged. On Thursday, 75,000 people returned to their homes; another 24,500 were allowed to return on Friday. However, some homes are still without electricity or water. Local officials expect the rest of the people to return home tomorrow.

On the day the story was written, how many people were still out of their homes?

_____

B **Explain your answer to your classmates.**

TEST YOURSELF ✔

Role-play a conversation about a community protest. Partner A: Tell your partner that there was a protest yesterday. Explain why the protesters were upset.
Partner B: You don't know about the protest. You agree with the protesters. Explain why. Then change roles.

1 Get ready to read

A Which news source do you prefer: radio, TV, newspapers, magazines, or the Internet? Why?

B Read the definitions. Which word is the opposite of *rise*?

drop: (verb) to fall
figure: (noun) a number
poll: (noun) a set of questions used to get an idea of people's opinions

C Look at the title and the graph in the magazine article in 2A. What do you think the article is about? Circle *a* or *b*.

a. the percent of people who enjoy talking about the news
b. people and their news habits

2 Read and respond

A Read the article. What has changed over the last 10 years?

Americans and the News

Where do you get the news? Do you like local, network, or cable TV news? Do you read the newspaper or magazines? Do you get your news online, or do you listen to the news on the radio? How much time do you spend every day getting the news? These are just some of the questions Americans answered in a poll on news habits. The results may surprise you.

People's news habits changed between 1994 and 2004. One change that isn't a surprise is the rise in online news. In 2004, 29 percent of people in the U.S. reported that they regularly[1] got the news online. In 1994, that figure was under 2 percent. Over the same 10 years, the percent of people who regularly got the news from the newspaper dropped from 58 percent

[1]regularly: often; frequently; almost every day

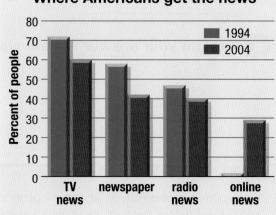

Where Americans get the news

☑ Use previewing skills to predict the content of a magazine article

to 42 percent. The percent of people who regularly got the news from the radio dropped from 47 percent to 40 percent.

Age makes a difference. Only 23 percent of people under 30 said that they have read a newspaper recently.

People also reported the amount of time they spent getting the news compared with the time they spent on other activities. The results showed that people spent more time getting the news than they spent watching non-news TV, reading, making personal phone calls, exercising, or shopping.

Technology may change, but one thing stays the same: people want to know what's going on.

Adapted from: *http://people-press.org*

B Listen and read the article again.

C Work with a partner. Ask and answer the questions.

1. What was the poll about?
2. Which news source became more popular from 1994 to 2004?
3. Which news sources became less popular?
4. Which news sources are most popular now?
5. Which news sources will be popular in the future?

3 Talk it over

Think about the questions. Talk about your ideas with the class.

1. Some people think that there is too much bad news on TV.
   Do you agree? Why?
2. Do you think that news reporters sometimes create news?
   If so, give an example.
3. Should parents and teachers talk to children about current events
   even if the news might upset them? Why or why not?

BRING IT TO LIFE

Read a local, national, or international news story in a newspaper or magazine, or on the Internet. Bring the article to class and talk about how the article answers the questions *who, what, where, when,* and *why.*

1 Grammar

A Rewrite the sentences in the past passive. Use *by* + noun when it is important to mention the person or thing performing the action.

1. A fire damaged two apartments in our building.

   <u>Two apartments in our building were damaged by a fire.</u>

2. Someone in the building pulled the fire alarm.

   _____

3. Two neighbors put the fire out.

   _____

4. Electrical problems caused two fires on our block last year.

   _____

5. The owners replaced the electrical system in the building.

   _____

B Read the answers. Complete the questions.

1. **A:** When <u>was the article about the protest written</u>?

   B: The article about the protest was written on Monday.

2. **A:** What _____?

   B: The protesters were called "neighborhood leaders" in the article.

3. **A:** Where _____?

   B: These pictures were taken at a club.

4. **A:** Why _____?

   B: The club was closed because neighbors protested.

C Complete the conversations. Use reflexive pronouns.

1. **A:** Did the teenagers clean the building <u>themselves</u>?

   B: Yes, they did. They bought the paint _____, too.

2. **A:** Why are you looking at _____ in the mirror?

   B: Because I gave _____ a haircut. How do I look?

   A: Ummm…, fine.

3. **A:** You and I should treat _____ to some ice cream.

   B: You go ahead. I'm on a diet.

   A: You're too hard on _____. You look great!

2 Group work

A Work with 2–3 classmates. Write a 6–8 line conversation between the people in the picture. Share your conversation with the class.

A: *Did you hear about...?*
B: *No, I didn't. What...?*

B Interview 3 classmates. Write their answers.

1. Where do you get the news? What do you like about your news source?
2. Do you think people have a responsibility to know about current events? Why or why not?
3. In your opinion, what have been the 3 most important events in the news this year?

C Talk about the answers with your class.

PROBLEM SOLVING

A Listen and read about Anton.

    Before Anton came to the United States, he always read the newspaper, watched the news on TV, and followed the international news on the Internet. He loved to talk to his friends about current events.

    However, since Anton came to the U.S., getting the news hasn't been so easy. He thinks it is very hard to understand TV and radio news in English. At work, his co-workers talk about current events at lunch. Anton would like to be able to talk about his opinions, too.

B Work with your classmates. Answer the questions.

1. What is Anton's problem?
2. What should Anton do? Think of 2 or 3 solutions to his problem.
3. Write a short letter to Anton. Tell him what you think he should do.

UNIT 3

Going Places

FOCUS ON
- travel problems and solutions
- using the telephone
- reported speech
- planning a trip
- cell-phone communication

LESSON 1 Vocabulary

1 Learn vocabulary for travel emergencies

A Talk about the questions with your class.

1. How do you like to travel—by car, by bus, or by train? Why?
2. What are some things you always take with you when you travel? Why?

B Work with your classmates. Match the words with the pictures.

_____ call the auto club	__1__ have a breakdown	_____ send a tow truck
_____ change a tire	_____ have a flat tire	_____ turn on the hazard lights
_____ get directions	_____ raise the hood	_____ use a safety triangle

C Listen and check. Then read the new words with a partner.

D Work with a partner. Write other travel emergency words you know. Check your words in a dictionary.

32   ☑ Identify and use travel emergency vocabulary to state problems and solutions

E Work with a partner. Ask and answer the questions. Use the words in 1B.

1. How do you know there is a travel emergency with the bus? With the cars?
2. What happened to the people in the pictures? What are they doing?

2 Learn vocabulary for travel problems

A Look at the pictures. Match the pictures with the statements.

out of gas   lost   stuck in traffic   locked out of the car

_d_ 1. She should call the auto club. She needs a locksmith.

_____ 2. He should walk to a gas station.

_____ 3. She should ask for directions.

_____ 4. He's going to be late. He should call his boss.

B Work with a partner. Practice the conversation. Use the words in 2A.

A: I can't believe this!

B: What's the problem?

A: I'm locked out of my car. What should I do?

B: You should call the auto club.

C Talk about the questions with your class.

1. What problems have you had while traveling by car or bus? What did you do?
2. What should you do if you have a car problem while you are driving?

> **TEST YOURSELF** ✔
> Close your book. Categorize the new words in two lists: *Travel Emergencies and Problems* and *Solutions*. Check your spelling in a dictionary. Compare your lists with a partner.

1 Read about using the phone

A Look at the pictures. Talk about the questions with your class.

1. Who do you think each person is calling?
2. How do the people feel? Why?

Please press one for road assistance...

Please leave a message at the tone...

B Listen and read the story.

	How I Made Friends with the Phone
	by Ahmed Bell
	When I first came to this country, it was very difficult for me to
	use the phone. I could understand people in person, but listening to
	people on the phone was a different story. I remember the first time
	I called about a job. The secretary said, "Can you hold?" and I said,
	"Hold what?" I didn't know that "hold" can mean "wait".
	My worst phone problem was automated messages with choices
	or menus. When I called the bank, for example, I couldn't understand
	the computer voice, and I couldn't get the information I needed.
	Sometimes, I called offices at night when the offices were closed. I
	could listen to their automated messages for English practice.
	Now, using the phone is much easier for me. I enjoy making phone
	calls, and I like it when people call me.

> **Writer's note**
>
> To repeat a speaker's words, add a comma (,) and quotation marks (" ").

C Check your understanding. Circle the correct words.

1. When the writer first came to the U.S., using the phone was (impossible / (very hard)).
2. He (could / couldn't) understand most people when he spoke to them in person.
3. He didn't understand a secretary when she asked him to (call again / wait).
4. He learned how to understand automated messages by (listening / leaving messages).

☑ Describe and report on experiences using the phone

2 Write about using the phone

A Talk about the questions with your class.

1. How is speaking in English on the phone different from communicating in person?
2. Do you get nervous when you have to use the phone? Why or why not?

B Write about your phone experience. Use the model in 1B and the questions below to help you.

Paragraph 1: When you first came to the U.S., was it difficult to understand English on the phone? Give an example of something you didn't understand.

Paragraph 2: What was your worst phone experience? What happened? How did you get better at using the phone?

Paragraph 3: How do you feel about using the phone now?

> My Worst Phone Experience
>
> When I first came to the U.S., it was difficult for me
> to use the phone. I couldn't understand...

C Use the checklist to edit your writing. Check (✔) the true sentences.

Editing checklist	
1. I wrote about the past and the present.	
2. I wrote about one of my experiences using the phone.	
3. I used the simple past to write about the past.	
4. I used a comma and quotation marks to repeat a speaker's words.	

D Exchange stories with a partner. Read and comment on your partner's work.

1. Point out one sentence that you think is interesting.
2. Ask your partner a question about his or her phone experience.

TEST YOURSELF ✔

Write a new story about another communication problem you had in English—on the phone or talking to someone in person.

1 Learn reported speech

A Look at the pictures. Where is Monty? Where are his friends?

Monty

I'm stuck in traffic.

Monty's friends

Monty called. He said he was stuck in traffic.

B Study the charts. Circle the example of reported speech in 1A.

REPORTED SPEECH WITH STATEMENTS

Quoted speech
Monty said, "**I'm stuck** in traffic."
Lia said, "**I'm waiting** for a tow truck."
They said, "**We don't have** a map."

Reported speech	
He said	(that) **he was** stuck in traffic.
She said	(that) **she was waiting** for a tow truck.
They said	(that) **they didn't have** a map.

Notes
• Use reported speech to tell what someone said or wrote.
• For quoted speech in the simple present, the reported speech is in the simple past.
• For quoted speech in the present continuous, the reported speech is in the past continuous.

C Fred invited his friends to dinner, but some of them called because they had problems getting to his home. What did they say? Complete the sentences with reported speech.

1. Luis said, "I'm lost."

   Luis said that ___he was lost_____.

2. Dora said, "The bus is stuck in traffic."

   Dora said _____.

3. Alice and Kim said, "We don't know the address."

   Alice and Kim said _____.

4. Sarah said, "I'm looking for a parking space."

   Sarah said that _____.

D Get the form. Work with your class. Correct the sentences.

Ali called this morning.

1. He said that he is on Elk Road.   <u>He said that he was on Elk Road.</u>

2. He says he was calling from a gas station.   _____

3. He said that he has a flat tire.   _____

4. He said he is going to be late.   _____

2 Learn reported speech with *told* + noun or pronoun

A Study the charts. Is Lee a man or a woman? How do you know?

REPORTED SPEECH WITH *TOLD* + NOUN OR PRONOUN

Quoted speech		Reported speech	
		Bob said	
Bob said, "Lee, **I have** a flat tire."		Bob told **Lee**	(that) **he had** a flat tire.
		Bob told **her**	
They said, "**We're waiting** for the bus."		They said	(that) **they were waiting** for the bus.
		They told **me**	

Notes
• Use *said* to report a person's words.
• Use *told* to report a person's words and to report on who the person is speaking to.
• Use a noun (*Lee*, etc.) or an object pronoun (*her, me*, etc.) after *told*.

B Complete the sentences with *said* or *told*.

1. Bob __said__ he was changing his tire.

2. Yan _____ Lisa that she didn't belong to an auto club.

3. The teacher _____ us that there was a car in the parking lot with its lights on.

4. My friends _____ they wanted to buy a new car.

C Look at the quoted speech. Complete the reported speech. Use object pronouns.

1. Mr. Ruiz stopped Liz in the hall. He said, "I need the key to the closet."
   Mr. Ruiz told <u>her that he needed the key to the closet</u>.

2. Tia phoned John. She said, "I'm calling about the homework."
   Tia told _____.

3. Ken emailed his parents. He said, "I'm taking driving lessons."
   Ken told _____.

4. Tasha called my sister and me. She said, "I'm locked out of my apartment."
   Tasha told _____.

3 Grammar listening

Listen to the conversations. Write the missing words.

1. David said that _____ he was _____ lost.
2. Patricia said that _____ a flat tire.
3. Gina said that _____ for a tow truck.
4. Sam and Joe said that _____ in traffic.
5. They said that _____ the bus.
6. Cindy said that _____ a cell phone.
7. Hank said that _____ to class.

    He also said that _____ out of gas.
8. Maria said that _____ a map.

4 Practice reported speech

A **Work with your classmates. Ask your classmates these questions. Take notes on their answers.**

1. Do you have a car?
2. What's your favorite form of transportation?
3. Do you like to travel?
4. Are you planning to take a trip soon?

B **Work with a partner. Tell your partner what your classmates said.**

A: *Max said that he had a used car.*
B: *June told me that she didn't have a car.*

TEST YOURSELF ✔

Close your book. Write 5 sentences about things your partner told you in 4B. Use reported speech with *told* or *said*.

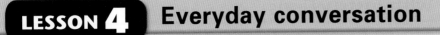

1 Learn to make travel plans

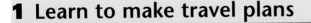

A Look at the ads. Listen to the conversations. Then answer the questions below with your classmates.

1. What website does Artie recommend?
2. Where does Rhonda think her friend should stay?

B Listen and read. Who knows more about planning a trip—A or B?

A: I'm planning a trip to Florida. I've never been there before.

B: Great. Do you have a hotel reservation?

A: No, I don't. My sister told me to use the Internet.

B: That's a good idea. If I were you, I'd try *hotels.int*.

A: Is it hard to use?

B: It's easy, and I'll bet* you can get a good price. Why don't you try it?

A: OK, I will. Thanks for the advice.

*Idiom note: I'll bet (OR I bet) = I'm sure

> **In other words...**
>
> **Making suggestions**
> If I were you, I'd...
> Why don't you...?
> You could...
> How about trying...?

C Role-play a conversation about planning a trip with a partner. Use the example in 1B to make a new conversation.

Partner A: You are planning to drive to San Francisco for the first time. You need directions. A friend told you to use a map website. Ask if it's hard to use.

Partner B: You agree that a map website is a good idea. Recommend *drivethere.map*. Explain that it's easy, and you can get maps and travel tips.

2 Learn reported speech with instructions

 A Study the charts. Do you use *said* or *told* with *me* for reported instructions?

REPORTED SPEECH WITH INSTRUCTIONS

Quoted Speech
Laila said, "Use a map website."
Mati said, "Don't take Highway 75."
Tomas said, "Please drive."

Reported Speech
Laila **told me to use** a map website.
Mati **told me not to take** Highway 75.
Tomas **said to drive**.

Note
Use an infinitive (*to* + verb OR *not to* + verb) to report an instruction.

B Work with a partner. Look at the pictures. Report Pedro and Lois' instructions.

1. <u>Pedro told Lois to call him every day.</u>
2. _____
3. _____
4. _____

3 Practice your pronunciation

 A Listen to the pronunciation of the letter *s* in these sentences.

Pronounced *s*	Pronounced *z*
Try thi<u>s</u> web<u>s</u>ite.	It i<u>s</u> ea<u>s</u>y to u<u>s</u>e.

B Work with a partner. How do you think the letter s is pronounced in these words? Circle s or z.

1. use	s	(z)	3. sister	s	z	5. cats	s	z
2. hotels	s	z	4. please	s	z	6. does	s	z

C Listen and check. Then read the words with a partner.

4 Focus on listening

A **Talk about the questions with your class.**

1. Where do you hear: *Press 1 for…, Press 2 for…*, etc.?
2. Are automated messages easy or difficult for you to follow or understand? Why?

B **Listen to the automated message. Check (✔) 2 things you can't do on this message system.**

☐ Make a reservation. ☐ Get information about jobs.
☐ Get room service. ☐ Find a nearby hotel.
☐ Order a wedding cake. ☐ Hear the message again.

C **Listen again. Write the numbers or the symbols the people should press.**

1. Omar wants to have a company meeting at a Motel 22. __3__
2. Elena wants to find a Motel 22 near her home. _____
3. Billy wants a reservation at the Motel 22 in Dallas, Texas. _____
4. Juanita needs to hear the choices again. _____
5. Kevin is looking for a job at a Motel 22. _____

5 Real-life math

A **Read the confirmation email for a hotel reservation and answer the questions.**

1. How many nights is Billy planning to stay at the Motel 22? _____
2. How much is Billy's room per night (room rate plus taxes and charges)? _____
3. What will be the total cost of his stay at Motel 22? _____

B **Explain your answers to your classmates.**

Email - Message (Plain Text)

File Edit View Insert Format Tools Actions Help

Reply | Reply to All | Forward | Print | Save | Delete

From: reservations@motel22
To: blewis@fince.ma
Subject: Your reservation
Date: 9/1

Dear Billy Lewis:
We are pleased to confirm your reservation at Motel 22. Please check the summary below. We look forward to seeing you!

Location: Motel 22, 1800 Clark Ave., Dallas, TX
Check-in (arrive): Wed, 10/14 [3 p.m.]
Check-out (leave): Friday, 10/16 [12 p.m.]
Room Rate: $79.00 per night;
Taxes and Charges: $8.55 per night
To modify or cancel this reservation, please call us at 1-800-555-2222.

TEST YOURSELF ✔

Role-play a conversation about making travel arrangements. Partner A: You want to take a trip for the weekend, but you're not sure where you want to go, how you should travel, or where to stay. Partner B: You always use the Internet to plan your trips. Give your friend advice. Then change roles.

1 Get ready to read

A Do you use a cell phone? How have cell phones changed the way people communicate?

B Read the definitions. Which word means *become bigger*?

get in touch with: [verb] to contact, talk or write to
increase: [verb] to get larger; grow
mobility: [noun] the ability to move around, or travel, easily
wireless: [adj.] without wires

C Scan the first paragraph of the magazine article in 2A. Then mark the sentences T (true) or F (false).

_____ 1. More than 50 percent of people in the U.S. carry cell phones.

_____ 2. From 1994 to 2004, the number of cell phones in the U.S. increased from 24 million to 80 million.

2 Read and respond

A Read the article. Why do people have cell phones?

Our Love–Hate Relationship with Cell Phones

Cell phones are a fact of modern life. More than 50 percent of people in the U.S. carry them. From 1994 to 2004, the number of cell phones in the U.S. increased from 24 million to 180 million.

Why do people have cell phones? When researchers asked this question, most people said that they wanted to be more accessible,[1] that they wanted to have greater mobility, or that a cell phone made them feel safe. Cell phones allow us to spend more time talking to family and friends. We use them on the go—when we are waiting in line or walking the dog. And they do make us feel safer. We know that we can get in touch with each other in case of an emergency.

[1] accessible: easy to talk to; easy to reach

  Interpret a magazine article on cell phones; scan an article for numbers

Cell phones have changed our lives and our ideas of politeness and privacy. Most of us don't enjoy listening to other people's phone conversations in public places, but we don't always have a choice. Cell-phone calls interrupt our conversations and can disturb the people around us. When we get a call in the middle of a face-to-face conversation, we have to make a decision about who to talk to, and that decision can hurt people's feelings.

Cell phones can cause problems, but they have real advantages when they're used for the right reasons. Whether you love cell phones or hate them, we can probably all agree that wireless communication is here to stay.

Source: *www.CTIA-The Wireless Association®*

B Listen and read the article again.

C Work with a partner. Answer the questions with information from the article.

1. What are two situations in which people often use cell phones?
2. What are two situations in which it is not polite to use cell phones?

D Study the chart. Complete the sentences with the correct words.

Word Study: The suffix *-less*			
Add *–less* to the end of some nouns to form adjectives.			
Word	**Meaning**	**Word**	**Meaning**
wireless	without a wire	harmless	not harmful or dangerous
useless	without a use; not useful	speechless	unable to speak

1. A cell phone is __useless__ if you forget to charge the battery.
2. _____ communication, such as cell phones, is common today.
3. When he called, I couldn't think of what to say. I was _____ with surprise.
4. My co-worker thinks cell phones are dangerous, but experts say they're _____.

3 Talk it over

Think about the question. Talk about your ideas with the class.

Many people say that they cannot imagine life without a cell phone.
Do you feel the same way? Why or why not?

BRING IT TO LIFE

Use the newspaper, the Internet, or store flyers to find information on cell-phone calling plans. Bring your information to class. Compare services with your classmates. Which plans have the best services?

STUDENT AUDIO

1 Grammar

A Complete the sentences. Use reported speech.

1. Patty said, "I need directions to the bus station."

   Patty said that _____.

2. She also said, "I want to use a map website."

   She also told me that _____.

3. Her co-workers said, "We don't know the zip code for the bus station."

   Her co-workers told her that _____.

B Read the reported speech. What did the speakers say? Write the quoted speech.

1. Abram said that he didn't understand his cell-phone bill.

   Abram said, "_____."

2. Eddy's mother said Eddy was staying home today.

   Eddy's mother said, "_____."

3. Sandra and her roommate said they had a new phone number.

   Sandra and her roommate said, "_____."

C Complete the sentences with *him, her, us,* or *them.*
Use the words in parentheses.

1. We told __them__ to meet us here. (Aldo and Mary)

2. They told _____ that they were locked out of their car. (Mrs. Ikito)

3. Ms. Ikito told _____ that they were waiting for the auto club. (my family and me)

4. I told _____ that Aldo and Mary needed an extra set of keys. (Mr. Ikito)

5. We told _____ where Aldo and Mary were waiting. (Mr. and Mrs. Ikito)

D Change the instructions to reported speech.

1. "Please call a tow truck," Ms. Holton said to her husband.

   Ms. Holton told him to call a tow truck.

2. "Stop at the intersection," Ali said to the taxi driver.

   _____

3. "Turn on the hazard lights," Gina said to Mrs. Perlas.

   _____

4. "Don't forget the map," my brother said to his friends.

   _____

2 Group work

A Work with 2–3 classmates. Write a 6–8 line conversation between the people in the picture. Eve is asking about Lin. Sue is reporting what Lin told her. Share your conversation with the class.

Eve: *Is Lin OK? What did she say?*
Sue: *She…*

B Interview 3 classmates. Write their answers.

1. When you travel, do you like to go somewhere new or somewhere you've visited before? Why?
2. What is the best travel advice you have ever heard? Why?
3. What are 3 things every traveler should know before leaving home?

C Talk about the answers with your class.

PROBLEM SOLVING

 A Listen and read about Kofi.

Kofi needs to make a trip to another city for a job interview. The airfare would be about $400 roundtrip. He wants to drive because he thinks it will be cheaper. Kofi is worried about his car, though. It broke down last week, and he had to pay a mechanic $200 to fix it. It's running all right now, but the car is more than 10 years old. He wants to be sure he won't have another breakdown on his trip. His car also needs new tires. New tires would cost about $500. Kofi has $800 in the bank.

B Work with your classmates. Answer the questions.

1. What is Kofi's problem?
2. What could he do? Think of 2 or 3 solutions to his problem.
3. Write a short letter to Kofi. Tell him what you think he should do.

Get the Job

FOCUS ON
• career planning resources
• writing a cover letter
• the past perfect
• job interviews
• making a career plan

LESSON **1** Vocabulary

1 Learn career-planning vocabulary

A Talk about the questions with your class.

1. Think about your future. What kind of work would you like to do?
2. What are some ways you can get more information about this kind of work?

B Work with your classmates. Match the words with the picture.

__1__ apply for financial aid   ____ take an interest inventory

____ look at job listings   ____ take a training class

____ see a career counselor   ____ use the resource center

 C Listen and check. Then read the new words with a partner.

D Work with a partner. Write other career planning words you know. Check your words in a dictionary.

✔ Identify and use career-planning vocabulary to discuss job-training opportunities

E Work with a partner. Practice the conversation. Use the words in 1B.

A: Good morning. Can I help you?

B: Yes, please. Is this where I sign up to use the resource center?

A: Yes, it is. Have a seat, and someone will be right with you.

2 Learn more career-planning vocabulary

A Look at the flyer. What kinds of training opportunities are available?

Ames Career Preparation Program
FALL TRAINING OPPORTUNITIES

Try a **Vocational Class**

Computer Repair | Auto Mechanics

Many other classes available.

Try a **Job-Skills Workshop**

Starting a job search?
This workshop will help.
Wednesday: 7 to 9 p.m.

Try an **Internship**

Internships give students valuable work experience. For information, call 555-1188.

Try a **Self-Study Course**

Teach yourself to type with a self-study course! Use our software in your home!

Try On-the-Job Training

Get training at your workplace. Information session, Thursday, Oct. 21, at 8 p.m.

Try an **Online Course**

Courses in Math and Writing. Learn online at your convenience!

MATH 101

B Work with a partner. Complete the sentences. Use the words in 2A.

1. Loc wants a promotion. He should ask his boss about _____on-the-job training_____.

2. Brenda likes using the Internet. She should try an _____.

3. Joe needs work experience. He should ask about an _____.

4. Mai has always wanted to be a mechanic. She could take a _____.

5. Tonio is starting to look for work. He should go to a _____.

6. Mira stays at home with her children. She could try a _____.

C Talk about the questions with your class.

1. What would you like to do at a career center? Why?

2. Think of a job or career you would like to have. How could you prepare for it?

TEST YOURSELF ✔

Close your book. Work with a partner. Make a list of as many new words from the lesson as you can. Alphabetize your list. Then check your spelling in a dictionary.

1 Read a cover letter

A Look at the cover letter. Talk about the questions with your class.

1. What is a cover letter?
2. Who do people send a cover letter to?

B Listen and read the cover letter.

Mr. Luis Sanchez
2394 Geneva Avenue, #443 ◄
Bayside, FL 34748
(836) 555-3992
lsanchez@cobe.net
July 26, 2007

Ms. Lee Porter
Director, Human Resources ◄
Vanit's Department Store, Inc.
1000 Oleander Drive
Bayside, FL 34748

Dear Ms. Porter:

This letter is in response to your job listing at the Ames Career Center for a customer service representative. I am enclosing my resume.

I have two years' experience as a cashier, and I've completed a training class in customer skills. My computer skills are excellent, and I am fluent in English and Spanish. I am reliable, organized, and hardworking.

I would like very much to meet with you. I have listed my contact information above. Thank you for considering me for this position.

Sincerely yours,
Luis Sanchez
Luis Sanchez

> **Writer's note**
>
> In a business letter, include your contact ●information and the job title and address of the person you are writing to.

C Check your understanding. Mark the sentences T (true), F (false), or NI (no information).

__T__ 1. Luis is applying for a job at Vanit's.

____ 2. Luis is writing to Ms. Porter because he met her at a job skills workshop.

____ 3. Luis doesn't know how to use a cash register.

____ 4. In his cover letter, Luis says why he is a good person for the job.

____ 5. Luis has applied for several jobs.

2 Write a cover letter

A **Look at the classified ad. Talk about the questions with your class.**

1. Would you like to apply for one of these jobs? If so, which one? If not, why not?
2. Think of a company in your area that you would like to work for. What job would you like to apply for?

> ## Help Wanted
>
> Bayside Health. **Nursing Aide**. No exp. req.; good English a must. **Front Desk Clerk**. Exp. with the public req. **Computer Technician**. PT, exp. preferred. Send resume to Ms. Larai Ondo, Human Resources Director, 11475 Elm St., Bayside, FL 34747, or ondo@bayh.fl. No calls, please.

B **Write a cover letter to Bayside Health or another company. Use the model in 1B and the questions below to help you.**

To start: What is your contact information?
Who are you writing to? What is the person's title and address?
Paragraph 1: What job are you applying for? What are you sending?
Paragraph 2: What are your qualifications (your education and experience)?
Paragraph 3: What would you like to do? How can the employer contact you?
To end: Sign your letter.

> (your contact information)
> (person's name, title, and address)
> Dear...
> This letter...

C **Use the checklist to edit your writing. Check (✔) the true sentences.**

Editing checklist	
1. I included my contact information and the title and address of the person I am writing to.	
2. My letter explains why I am writing.	
3. I described my experience, skills, and personal characteristics.	
4. I signed my letter.	

D **Exchange letters with a partner. Read and comment on your partner's work.**

1. Point out one sentence that you think will help your partner get an interview.
2. Ask your partner a question about his or her qualifications.

TEST YOURSELF ✔

Write a new cover letter for another job from 2A.

1 Learn the past perfect

A **Read the story about Luis. What did he do before and after his interview?**

On Thursday, Luis Sanchez got a phone call from Ms. Porter at Vanit's Department store. She had read Luis' resume, and she wanted to interview him at 3:00 that afternoon.

When Luis arrived for the interview, he had already read some information about the company, and he had planned some questions to ask. He hadn't completed an application. He did that while he was waiting.

When the interview was over, Luis felt that he'd done well. Later, he wrote Ms. Porter a thank-you note.

B **Study the chart and the time line. Underline the 5 past perfect verbs in 1A.**

THE PAST PERFECT

Affirmative and negative statements		
Subject	*had/had not* + past participle	
He	**had planned**	some questions before he arrived.
He	**hadn't completed**	an application before he arrived.

The Past Perfect
past   now ◄———✕————————————✕————————┼————► Ms. Porter read   Ms. Porter called Luis. Luis' resume.

Note
Use the past perfect to show that an event happened before another event in the past. The past perfect shows the earlier event. 　　Ms. Porter **had read** Luis' resume before she called him. 　　(First Ms. Porter read Luis' resume. Then she called him.)

C **Complete the sentences with the past perfect form of the verbs in parentheses.**

1. Ms. Porter called Luis after she _____had read_____ his resume. (read)

2. On Tuesday, Luis was worried because Ms. Porter _____ him. (not call)

3. Luis _____ at Vanit's website when Ms. Porter called him. (not look)

4. Luis _____ some questions before he went to the interview. (prepare)

5. A career counselor _____ Luis some advice before the interview. (give)

D Get the meaning. Work with your class. What happened first? Circle *a* or *b*.

1. When I started the training class, I had already tried a self-study course.
   a. I started a training class.
   b. I tried a self-study course.

2. Unfortunately, we arrived after the counselor had left.
   a. The counselor left.
   b. We arrived.

3. After I sat down, I realized that I had forgotten to sign in.
   a. I sat down.
   b. I forgot to sign in.

2 Learn past perfect questions

A Study the charts. What verb is used in the short answers?

PAST PERFECT QUESTIONS

Yes/No questions
A: **Had** you **sent** a resume before you called?   B: Yes, I **had.** OR   No, I **hadn't.**
A: **Had** all the applicants **sent** resumes?   B: Yes, they **had.** OR   No, they **hadn't.**

Information questions
A: How many jobs **had** you **applied** for before you got this job?   B: I had applied for two jobs before I got this job.
A: Which classes **had** they **taken** before they started their internships?   B: They had taken computer classes before they started their internships.

B Look at the answers. Then complete the questions with the past perfect.

1. A: What _had you looked at_ before you applied for the job?

   B: Before I applied for the job, I had looked at the company's website.

2. A: _____ the training class before he applied for the job?

   B: Yes, he had. Pietro finished the training class two weeks ago.

3. A: How many people _____ before you?

   B: I don't know how many people they had interviewed before me.

4. A: Why _____ to Vanit's before she applied
      for the job there?

   B: She had gone to Vanit's to shop before she applied for the job there.

5. A: _____ in an office before you applied
      for the internship?

   B: No, I hadn't. I had worked in a restaurant, but not in an office.

3 Grammar listening

 Listen to Mopati talk about his life. Circle the correct words.

1. Before Mopati came to the U.S., he had always lived in a
   (small town /(big city)).
2. Now he lives in a (small town / big city).
3. Before Mopati came to the U.S., he had studied (French / English).
4. Now he studies (French / Spanish).
5. Before Mopati came to the U.S., he had always wanted to be a
   (teacher / businessman).
6. Now he wants to be a (teacher / businessman).

4 Practice the past perfect

A **Think about your answers to these questions.**

1. What are two things you'd never seen
   before you came to the U.S.?
2. What is one thing you'd never done
   before you came to the U.S.?
3. What's one word you'd never heard
   before you started this class?

B **Work with a partner. Ask and answer the questions.**

A: *What are two things you'd never done
   before you came to the U.S.?*
B: *I'd never…*

C **Talk about your ideas with the class.**

Before Franco came to the U.S., he had never…

TEST YOURSELF ✔

Close your book. Write 4 sentences about your partner's answers. Use the
past perfect.

---

1 Learn to respond to interview questions

A Look at the pictures. Listen to the conversations. Then answer the questions below with your classmates.

Ms. Jones

Ms. Adams

1. Whose interview is longer—Ms. Jones' or Ms. Adams'? Why?
2. In your opinion, which applicant does the interviewer think is better? Why?

B Listen and read. Do you think Luis will get the job?

Ms. Porter:	Tell me about yourself, Mr. Sanchez. Have you had much experience?
Luis:	Do you mean with customers?
Ms. Porter:	Yes, and other work experience, too.
Luis:	Well, I've been a cashier in a convenience store for two years. Before that, I worked as a stock clerk.
Ms. Porter:	How about training?
Luis:	Well, I took a self-study course in customer skills last month. Before that, I'd already learned a lot about customer service on the job.
Ms. Porter:	Very good. You have just the skills we need.

> **In other words...**
>
> **Checking understanding**
> Do you mean...?
> You mean...?
> Is that...?

C Role-play an interview with a partner. Use the example in 1B to make a new conversation.

Partner A: You're the interviewer. Ask about the applicant's experience and training. Give the applicant positive feedback.

Partner B: You are interviewing for a job as an office manager. Listen to the interviewer's first question and check your understanding. Talk about your work experience. You've been an office assistant for six months; before that you were a file clerk for a construction company. You took a computer-skills class this year and an online course in office management last year.

2 Compare the simple past, the past perfect, and the present perfect

A Study the chart. Mark the statements below T (true) or F (false).

Simple past	Sam **got** his first job in a hospital in 1998. He **took** English classes from 1999 to 2002.
Past perfect	Sam **had** already **taken** a training class when he got the job, but he **hadn't worked** in a hospital before.
Present perfect	Sam **has worked** at the hospital since 1998. He **has learned** a lot of English at his job.

__F__ 1. Sam hasn't learned to speak English yet.

_____ 2. Sam had already gotten his job before he started English classes.

_____ 3. Sam got the job and then took a training class.

_____ 4. Sam is still a hospital worker.

B Work with a partner. Circle the correct words.

I deliver letters and packages by bicycle. ((I've had) / I had) this job for three months, and I
$\qquad$ (1)
like it a lot. (I'd worked / I've worked) as a delivery driver before (I've gotten / I got)
$\qquad$ (2) $\qquad$ (3)
this job, but (I didn't like / I haven't liked) driving all day. On my bicycle,
$\qquad$ (4)
(I've learned / I learned) a lot more about the city. I also get a lot more exercise—
$\qquad$ (5)
(I've lost / I lost) ten pounds already!
$\qquad$ (6)

C Work with a partner. Ask and answer the questions.

1. Are you working now? If so, how long have you worked at your present job?
2. Had you worked before you got this job? If so, what did you like about that job?

3 Practice your pronunciation

A Listen. Notice how speaker B uses rising intonation to check understanding.

1. A: Tell me about your experience.
   B: Do you mean in construction? ↗

2. A: What were your responsibilities?
   B: You mean at my last job? ↗

B Practice the conversations with a partner. Use rising intonation to check understanding. Then listen and check.

1. A: Tell me about your last job.
   B: My last job in an office?

2. A: What experience have you had?
   B: Experience in the U.S.?

3. A: Have you had any training?
   B: Computer training?

4. A: Do you have any questions?
   B: Questions about the job?

4 Focus on listening

A **Talk about the questions with your class.**

1. What is a resume for? What information is usually on a resume?
2. Have you ever written a resume? If so, when did you write it?

B **Listen to the conversation. Answer the questions.**

1. Is Hanna taking a training course now?
2. Has Hanna typed her resume yet?

C **Listen again. Circle the correct words.**

1. Hanna (has / (hasn't)) finished her training class yet.
2. For the training class, Liz tells Hanna to write the month she started the class to (now / present).
3. For her English class, Hanna should write the name of the school, the place, the name of the (teacher / class), and the year she studied there.
4. Hanna finished high school in (her country / the U.S.)

HANNA LEE
4482 THIRD STREET
AUSTIN TX 78701
(512) 555-1435
EDUCATION

5 Real-life math

A **Read part of Hanna's resume and answer the questions.**

1. How long had Hanna been a cashier before she became a home health-care aide?

   _____

2. How long did she work as a file clerk?

   _____

B **Explain your answers to your classmates.**

Employment history	
6/1/05 – present	Home health-care aide, Sunnyside Associates, Austin
11/1/03 – 5/31/05	Cashier, Tannelo Department Stores, Austin
9/1/99 – 4/28/03	File Clerk, Central Market Supplies, Austin

TEST YOURSELF ✔

Role-play a job interview. Decide on the job together. Partner A: You're the applicant. Answer the interviewer's questions. Partner B: You're the employer. Ask questions to find out your partner's qualifications for the job. Then change roles.

1 Get ready to read

 A **What do you think is the best way to find a good job?**

B **Read the definitions. Which word is something a student wants to receive?**

field: (noun) profession; area or subject of study or work

scholarship: (noun) money from the government or other group to help pay for school

variety: (noun) a number of different kinds of things

C **Look at the title and the headings in the article in 2A. What do you think the article is about?**

2 Read and respond

 A **Read the article. What are the three steps to finding a career?**

Career Planning: $teps to $uccess

Are you tired of the same old job, day after day? Are you ready for a career? Here are the steps to take.

1. Make a career plan.

➡ Make a list of your skills. Include your work skills (using a cash register, repairing cars), your life skills (using a computer, taking care of children, speaking different languages), and your "people skills" (working with others, communicating ideas).

➡ Make a list of interesting jobs or careers. If you can, take an interest inventory or a skills inventory to help you decide which career seems right for you. Find out which fields are expected to grow over the next ten years.

2. Improve your skills.

➡ After you've identified a career,[1] find out what education or training you need.

---
[1] identify a career: find or choose a career

Some careers, especially in medical or technical fields, require special training. A career counselor or a career website can help you find opportunities for training.

➡ Training can be expensive. Financial aid can help you pay. Financial aid options include scholarships, loans, and work-study programs.

3. Find the right job.

➡ Use a variety of job-search resources. Look for possible employers in the newspaper, on the Internet, or at a career center. Networking, or just talking to people, can also help.

➡ Be organized in your job search. Make notes every time you contact a company. Write down the names and job titles of people you talk to.

➡ Be patient. Finding the right job can take time, but it's worth it. Good luck!

Source: *www.acinet.org*

B **Listen and read the article again.**

C **Scan the article. Circle the correct words.**

1. Start a career plan by making a list of (your skills and interests / job resources).
2. The article says that taking care of children is a (life skill / people skill).
3. Choose a field that will probably (pay well / grow) over the next ten years.
4. Work-study programs are one example of (skills / financial aid).
5. When you network, you (take an interest inventory / talk to people).
6. The article says it's important to find (a job quickly / the right job).

D **Study the chart. Complete the sentences with the correct words.**

> **Word Study: Suffixes -er and -ee**
>
> Add -er to the end of some verbs to show the person who performs an action.
> Add -ee to the end of some verbs to show the person who receives the result of the action.
> An **employer** employs an **employee**.
>
> | Verb | Nouns | |
> |------|-------|--------|
> | employ | employer | employee |
> | train | trainer | trainee |
> | pay | payer | payee |

1. Ms. Adams has been an __employee__ here for several years. Her _____ thinks that she is an excellent worker.
2. Mr. Jonson is a computer _____. He has 15 _____ in his class right now.
3. The person who receives a check is the _____. The person who writes it is the _____.

3 Talk it over

Think about the questions. Talk about your ideas with the class.

1. What work skills do you have? What other skills do you have?
2. Think about people you know. How did they get their jobs?

> **BRING IT TO LIFE**
> Find a skills inventory or career-interest inventory at the library, at a career center, or on the Internet. Complete the inventory. What careers does it tell you to look at? Do you agree? Talk about your ideas with your classmates.

1 Grammar

A Read the situations. Write new sentences with the past perfect and *before*.

1. In May 2005, Yuri had three interviews at Calto, Inc. In July, the company offered him a job.

   Yuri had had three interviews at Calto, Inc. before the company offered him a job.

2. At 4 p.m., the interviewer called with good news. At 5 p.m., Leila got home.

   _____

3. On Tuesday, Rico took a skills inventory. On Wednesday, the career counselor met with him.

   _____

4. In the morning, Yolanda went to the company's website. In the afternoon, she wrote her cover letter.

   _____

B Read the applicant's answers. Write the career counselor's questions. Use the past perfect.

1. **A:** _How long had you worked in the factory before you left for the U.S.?_

   B: I had worked in the factory for two years before I left for the U.S.

2. **A:** _____

   B: Yes, I had. I had gone to a career center before I called you.

3. **A:** _____

   B: No, I hadn't taken a skills inventory before I came here.

4. **A:** _____

   B: I'd been here five times before I made this appointment.

C Complete the sentences. Use the past perfect or the present perfect of the verbs in parentheses.

1. Mahmoud _____had_____ already _____accepted_____ another job when Ms. Simms called him. (accept)

2. Alice _____ a lot about working with people in her present job. (learn)

3. I _____ two online courses since I got my GED. (take)

4. Donata _____ as a translator before she came to this country. (work)

5. Irene _____ never _____ about a career in sales before she got her present job as a salesperson. (think)

2 Group work

 A **Work with 2–3 classmates. Write a 6–8 line conversation between the people in the picture. Share your conversation with the class.**

A: *Tell me something about your experience.*
B: *Well,…*

B **Interview 3 classmates. Write their answers.**

1. Before you came to the U.S., what kind of career training had you had?
2. Before we talked about career planning in this class, had you ever made a list of your skills? Why or why not?
3. In your opinion, what is the most important thing people should do at a job interview?

C **Talk about the answers with your class.**

PROBLEM SOLVING

 A **Listen and read about Jin.**

Jin works in her family's restaurant. She's worked there for three years, and she's very good at her job. She has learned to cook, wait on customers, use the cash register, and keep track of the restaurant's accounts. Jin likes helping her family, but she is thinking about her future. Before her family decided to come to the U.S., she had studied accounting at a technical school. Jin would like to work in the accounting field, but she doesn't know how to look for a job. She's never written a resume or gone on a job interview.

B **Work with your classmates. Answer the questions.**

1. What is Jin's problem?
2. What do you think Jin should do? Think of 2 or 3 solutions to her problem.
3. Write a short letter to Jin. Tell her what you think she should do.

UNIT 5

Safe and Sound

FOCUS ON
- dangers, warnings, safety precautions
- preparing for an emergency
- modals of advice and warning
- giving warnings
- injuries on the job and at home

LESSON 1 **Vocabulary**

1 Learn vocabulary for safety hazards and warnings

A **Talk about the questions with your class.**

1. Where do you see safety or warning signs?
2. What safety or warning signs have you seen at or near your school?

B **Work with your classmates. Match the words with the picture.**

____ broken ladder	____ frayed cord	_1_ restricted area
____ corrosive chemicals	____ poisonous fumes	____ slippery floor
____ flammable liquids	____ radioactive materials	

 C **Listen and check. Then read the new words with a partner.**

D **Work with a partner. Write other words you know for safety hazards and warnings. Check your words in a dictionary.**

E Work with a partner. Practice the conversations. Use the words in 1B.

1. **A:** Be careful! That floor is slippery!   2. **A:** Watch out! Those fumes are poisonous.

   B: OK, thanks.   **B:** Oh, OK. Thanks for the warning.

2 Learn vocabulary for safety precautions

A Look at the safety poster. Where do you think you might you see this poster?

Four Ways to Be Safe on Campus

Be Alert
Keep your eyes open. Watch for anything unusual in the area around you.

Avoid Isolated Areas
Walk in areas where there are people around you, especially at night.

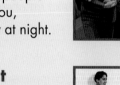

Report Suspicious Activities Immediately
If you see something, tell someone about it.

Prevent Accidents
Follow all safety rules, and report dangerous situations.

B Match the safety advice with the examples.

_c_ 1. Be alert.   a. You report broken equipment.

____ 2. Report suspicious activities.   b. You walk along a busy street.

____ 3. Avoid isolated areas.   c. You notice the door to a building is unlocked.

____ 4. Prevent accidents.   d. Someone is entering a building through a window.

C Talk about the questions with your class.

1. Which of the safety hazards, warning signs, or situations from this lesson have you seen at home? At work? At school? Describe one situation or hazard.
2. How can people prevent accidents at home? At work? At school?
3. Which things in your home have warning or caution labels?

TEST YOURSELF ✔

Work with a partner. Partner A: Read the vocabulary words in 1B to your partner. Partner B: Close your book. Write the words. Ask your partner for help with spelling as necessary. Then change roles. Partner B: Use the words in 2B.

1 Read about emergency preparations

A Talk about the questions with your class.

1. What types of weather emergencies occur in your area?
2. Have you ever made an emergency plan?
   Why or why not?

> **Need help?**
>
> **Weather emergencies**
>
> | | |
> |---|---|
> | blizzard | hurricane |
> | drought | tornado |
> | flood | |

B Listen and read the emergency plan.

	Hurricane Emergency Plan by the Duval Family
I.	Before
	A. Make emergency kit
	1. Supplies we have: canned food, can opener, blankets, radio
	2. Supplies to buy: batteries for radio, first-aid kit, bottled water, flashlight
	B. Get information
	1. Learn evacuation routes
	2. Identify emergency contact person
II.	During
	A. Stay safe
	1. Stay indoors and away from windows
	2. Don't use candles or electrical equipment
	B. Be aware
	1. Watch for tornadoes
	2. Listen for warnings
III.	After
	A. Check radio or TV for instructions
	B. Check house for damage

> **Writer's note**
>
> Use phrases or short sentences when you make an outline. You don't have to use articles (*a, an, the*) or ending punctuation.

C Check your understanding. Mark the statements **T** (true), **F** (false), or **NI** (no information).

_F_ 1. The Duval family already has a first-aid kit.

____ 2. The family needs to buy batteries.

____ 3. In the Duvals' area, tornadoes might occur during hurricanes.

____ 4. The Duvals live in Florida.

2 Write an emergency plan

A Talk about the questions with your class.

1. What types of emergencies do people in your area prepare for?
2. What steps should people take to prepare for different kinds of emergencies?
3. Where can you get information about possible emergencies in your area?

B Outline a plan for an emergency in your area. Use the model in 1B and the questions below to help you.

Part 1: What should you do before the emergency?
What do you have? What should you buy?
What information should you get?
Part 2: How can you stay safe during the emergency?
What should you be aware of?
Part 3: What should you do after the emergency?

> [Title]
> I. Before...
> A.
> B.
> II. During...
> A.
> B.
> III. After...
> A.
> B.

C Use the checklist to edit your writing. Check (✔) the true sentences.

Editing checklist	
1. I gave my plan a title.	
2. I included plans for before, during, and after an emergency.	
3. I followed the format for an outline.	
4. I used phrases or short sentences.	

D Exchange plans with a partner. Read and comment on your partner's work.

1. Point out one good idea for emergency preparation.
2. Ask your partner a question about his or her plan.

TEST YOURSELF ✔

Write a new outline for a plan for another possible emergency at your workplace or school.

1 Learn about necessity and prohibition

A Read the article. What does the city official say that people have to do?

City Official Says Silton Bay Must Prepare for Major Earthquake

City Official Sam Andreas announced that Silton Bay is not prepared for a major earthquake. Andreas said, "People think that they don't have to worry about a major earthquake here, but they're wrong."

According to Andreas, people have got to prepare. They have to buy emergency food and medical supplies. People also must make an emergency plan. They have to plan where to go if their homes are damaged. After an earthquake, damaged homes will be tagged with red tags. People must not enter a home with a red tag.

B Study the charts. Underline the 6 examples of *have to, have got to, must*, and *must not* in the article above.

HAVE TO, HAVE GOT TO, AND MUST FOR NECESSITY AND PROHIBITION

Necessity		
People	have to have got to must	prepare for emergencies.

Lack of necessity		
People in Florida	don't have to	prepare for earthquakes.

Prohibition		
After an earthquake, people	must not	enter a home with a red tag.

C Complete the sentences with *(don't) have to, have got to,* or *must not*.

1. You <u>must not</u> go out of the house during a hurricane.

2. I _____ buy any canned food. I have some already.

3. She _____ worry about floods. She lives in a safe area.

4. You _____ use electrical equipment during a hurricane. It's extremely dangerous.

5. The tornado is coming! You _____ go outside.

6. We _____ watch the news on TV. We can listen to it on the radio instead.

D Mark the statements N (necessary), NN (not necessary), or P (prohibited).

 _P_ 1. That chemical has poisonous fumes. You must not use it in the house.

____ 2. We've got to prepare for emergencies.

____ 3. You don't have to be afraid to walk at night when you walk with friends.

____ 4. We must fix the broken ladder before we use it.

____ 5. You must not stand by a window in a tornado.

2 Learn to express necessity in the past

A Study the chart. What words are used to express necessity in the past?

Necessity in the past	
Present	**Past**
This year, Rosa **has to** buy new supplies.	Last year, she **had to** buy a first-aid kit.
They'**ve got to** buy a new flashlight.	They **had to** buy a ladder last month.
Her husband **must** check the house for storm damage.	He **had to** repair the roof last November.
Their son **doesn't have to** go to school this week.	He **didn't have to** go to school last week.

Note
There are no past forms of *must* or *have got to* to express necessity. Use *had to* instead.

B Complete the sentences. Circle the correct words.

1. Rosa and her family (had to / have to) repair the roof last year.

2. Her husband (doesn't have to / didn't have to) replace the windows then.

3. Every year he (had to / has to) check the house for storm damage.

4. Now he (has got to / had to) replace the back door.

5. Their neighbor (had to / must) buy new furniture after the storm.

6. Now they (had to / must) make an emergency plan before the next big storm.

C Complete the sentences. Talk about your answers with a partner.

1. As a child when I was sick, I didn't have to _____.

2. One hundred years ago, when there was a hurricane, people probably
   had to _____.

3. Last week, I had to _____.

4. Last year, I had to _____.

5. Last year, I didn't have to _____.

3 Grammar listening

Listen to the emergencies. Choose the sentences with the same meaning. Circle *a* or *b*.

1. (a.) We have to call 911.
   b. We don't have to call 911.
2. a. We have got to evacuate the area.
   b. We don't have to evacuate the area.
3. a. Children must go to the basement.
   b. Children must not go to the basement.
4. a. They have to leave the area.
   b. They don't have to leave the area.
5. a. Last year, they had to leave the area.
   b. Last year, they didn't have to leave the area.
6. a. Most people had to buy emergency supplies.
   b. Most people didn't have to buy emergency supplies.

4 Practice expressing necessity and prohibition

A **Think about the answers to these questions.**

1. What are three things people have to do to prepare for an emergency?
2. What are three things people must not do when they are driving a car?
3. What are three things you've got to do to learn English?

B **Work with a partner. Ask and answer the questions.**

A: *What are three things people have to do to prepare for an emergency?*
B: *They have to buy emergency supplies...*

C **Talk about your ideas with the class.**

People have to buy emergency supplies.

TEST YOURSELF ✔

Close your book. Write 5 sentences about what people *have to do, must do,* and *don't have to do* in the situations you discussed in 4C.

---

1 Learn to report unsafe conditions

STUDENT
AUDIO

A Look at the picture. Listen to the conversations. Then ask and answer the questions below with your classmates.

1. What did the first employee report?
2. What did the second employee report?
3. What should people do in these situations?

STUDENT
AUDIO

B Listen and read. What safety hazards does the employee report?

A: Excuse me. I want to report a safety hazard.

B: Yes? What is it?

A: There are a lot of boxes in front of the emergency exit. That's dangerous.

B: You're right. The delivery workers should have put the boxes in the storeroom. I'll take care of it.* Thanks.

A: There's something else, too.

B: Oh? What's that?

A: There seems to be a problem with the back exit. The door won't close.

B: Thanks for bringing it to my attention. I'll call maintenance.

*Idiom note: take care of it = solve the problem

> **In other words...**
>
> **Reporting a problem**
> I want to report...
> There seem(s) to be...
> I noticed...

C Role-play a conversation about unsafe conditions with a partner. Use the example in 1B to make a new conversation.

Partner A: You're at the park. Tell a park employee about a safety hazard. There's broken glass near the playground. You also notice that the trash cans are full.

Partner B: You're a park employee. Listen to the visitor. You agree that someone should have cleaned up the glass. Tell the visitor you'll take care of the problems.

2 Learn *should have*

A Study the chart. Where are the boxes?

Should have	
Affirmative statements	**Negative statements**
You **should have put** the boxes in the storeroom. He **should have listened** to his manager.	You **should not have left** them in the hall. He **shouldn't have forgotten** the boxes.

Note
Use *should (not) have* + past participle to give an opinion about a situation in the past.

B Work with a partner. Write statements with *should have* or *shouldn't have*.

1. I didn't report the problem.

   You should have reported the problem.

2. We went into a restricted area.

   _____

3. They didn't wear protective gloves.

   _____

4. She used a lamp with a frayed cord.

   _____

5. He climbed on the broken ladder.

   _____

3 Practice your pronunciation

A Listen to the pronunciation of *-ough* in these words. Then match each word with *-ough* with a word that has a similar sound.

   b   1. bought   a. stuff

  _____ 2. through   b. saw

  _____ 3. enough   c. go

  _____ 4. though   d. too

B Read the conversation with a partner. Then listen and check your pronunciation.

A: I bought a new lock for the restricted area.

B: Do you think one lock is enough?

A: Yes, if we put it through the handles of both doors.

B: Good. We still need a lock for the supply cabinet, though.

4 Focus on listening

A Check (✔) the job you think is the safest. Talk about your answer with your class.

_____ teacher   _____ hotel worker   _____ computer technician

B Listen to the news story. Check (✔) the job that is NOT mentioned.

_____ librarian   _____ scientist   _____ telecommunications worker

_____ nurse   _____ teacher   _____ veterinarian

C Listen again. Mark the sentences T (true) or F (false).

__T__ 1. Teachers have a safer job than hotel workers.

_____ 2. It's a little safer to work in computers than in telecommunications.

_____ 3. Telecommunications workers have the safest jobs.

_____ 4. In the computer industry, workers have to work very slowly.

_____ 5. The injury/illness rate for scientists is 680 per 10,000.

5 Real-life math

A Read the chart about workplace safety. Then look at the groups of jobs below. Which group has the most illnesses and injuries?

Group 1: manufacturing jobs, construction jobs, transportation and warehouse jobs

Group 2: health-care and social-services jobs, retail jobs, hotel and vacation jobs

B Explain your answer to your classmates.

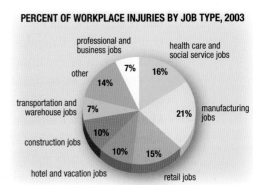

PERCENT OF WORKPLACE INJURIES BY JOB TYPE, 2003

professional and business jobs 7%
health care and social service jobs 16%
other 14%
transportation and warehouse jobs 7%
manufacturing jobs 21%
construction jobs 10%
hotel and vacation jobs 10%
retail jobs 15%

Source: *www.bls.gov*

TEST YOURSELF ✔

Role-play a conversation between a tenant and a superintendent about safety. Partner A: You noticed a dangerous situation in your apartment building. Tell the superintendent about the problem. Partner B: You are the superintendent. Listen and tell the tenant what you will do to solve the problem. Then change roles.

1 Get ready to read

A Name some jobs that are very dangerous. Which jobs are safe?

B Read the definitions. Have you ever had a sprain or a strain?

keep track of: (verb) to watch, keep a record of
sprain: (noun) an injury caused by suddenly twisting or turning a part of the body
strain: (noun) an injury caused by using a part of the body too much

C Scan the article. Check (✔) the most dangerous item in the home.

_____ cleaning materials   _____ exercise equipment   _____ basketballs

2 Read and respond

A Read the article. Which government agency keeps track of workplace injuries? Home injuries?

Accidents Can Happen Anywhere!

Accidents and injuries can happen at any time—at home or at work. Knowing which injuries are the most common can help employers, families, and individuals avoid and prevent them.

The U.S. Department of Labor keeps track of the amount of time people take off from work because of injuries and illnesses. In a recent survey, the Department of Labor found that sprains and strains were the most common reasons given for workers taking time off. Many of these injuries were back injuries caused by overexertion (too much hard physical work), accidents with equipment, or heavy lifting.

The home can be dangerous, too. Accidents happen when people are careless or when they don't use caution. Many injuries in the home are caused by everyday items. According to the U.S. Consumer Product Safety Commission, stairs and ramps are two of the most dangerous parts of the home. Bicycles, tools, and containers account for[1] many injuries that people go to emergency rooms for. However, a recent survey showed that the most dangerous item of all is the basketball!

[1]account for: to be responsible for

Number of Emergency Room Visits by Cause

Y-axis: Number of Visits — 0, 100,000, 200,000, 300,000, 400,000, 500,000, 600,000

Bars (left to right): basketballs; cans, bottles jars; exercise, exercise equipment; home workshop tools; toys; cleaning materials, equipment

X-axis: Cause of Injury

Injuries and accidents cannot be avoided completely, but knowing where the dangers are can help. As always, when it comes to staying safe, prevention is the best strategy.

adapted from: *www.bls.gov and www.cpsc.gov*

B Listen and read the article again.

C Check (✔) the main idea of the article.

_____ 1. Most jobs are not dangerous, but some jobs can be very dangerous.

_____ 2. More injuries happen in the home than in the workplace.

_____ 3. Both the workplace and home can be dangerous.

D Study the chart. Then circle the correct words in the sentences below.

> **Word Study: Forming adjectives from nouns**
>
> Add -*ous* to the end of some nouns to form adjectives. There is sometimes a spelling change: cautio**n**—cautio**us**
>
> | Noun | Adjective |
> |------|-----------|
> | caution | cautious |
> | danger | dangerous |
> | hazard | hazardous |

1. Don't leave things on the stairs. It's a safety (hazard / hazardous).
2. Be (caution / cautious) around flammable liquids. They're a (danger / dangerous) at many workplaces.
3. That frayed cord is very (danger / dangerous). These chemicals look (hazard / hazardous), too.

3 Talk it over

Think about the questions. Talk about your ideas with the class.

1. Which do you think is more dangerous, the home or the workplace? Why?
2. What kinds of safety training should employers give their workers?

BRING IT TO LIFE
Use the newspaper, a magazine, or the Internet to find an article on safety at home. What problems or hazards does the article talk about? What safety procedures does the article suggest? Talk about your article with your classmates.

1 Grammar

A Complete the sentences with *must not* or *don't have to*.

1. To prevent falls, you ___must not___ walk on a wet floor.
2. You _____ report that broken window. I already reported it.
3. People _____ forget to report safety hazards.
4. You _____ worry about emergencies if you're prepared.

B Read the information. Which sentences are closest in meaning? Circle *a* or *b*.

1. It's really important to use caution when you're going downstairs.
   a. You must be careful when you're going downstairs.
   b. You must not be careful when you're going downstairs.

2. You don't have to buy an emergency kit. It's fine to make one yourself.
   a. You've got to buy an emergency kit.
   b. It isn't necessary to buy an emergency kit.

3. It could be dangerous to go out by yourself. Wait until someone can go with you.
   a. You don't have to go out by yourself.
   b. You must not go out by yourself.

4. We're required to put new batteries in the smoke alarms next month.
   a. We must put new batteries in the smoke alarms this month.
   b. We don't have to put new batteries in the smoke alarms this month.

C Randy's back hurts. Write sentences with *should have* or *shouldn't have*.

1. He moved boxes for two hours on Saturday.
   He shouldn't have moved boxes for two hours on Saturday.

2. He didn't ask for help.

   _____

3. He played basketball on Sunday.

   _____

4. He lifted weights after he played basketball.

   _____

5. He didn't rest his back.

   _____

2 Group work

A Work with 2–3 classmates. Write a 6–8 line conversation between the people in the picture. Share your conversation with the class.

A: *We need to make a family emergency plan.*
B: *OK. What do we have to do first?*

B Interview 3 classmates. Write their answers.

1. What is the most dangerous or unsafe situation you've ever seen?
   Did you report it? If you did, what happened?
2. Is it easy for you to report a dangerous or unsafe situation? Why or why not?
3. What are some things people should take with them if they have to evacuate their homes? What are some things they don't have to take?

C Talk about the answers with your class.

PROBLEM SOLVING

 A Listen and read about Mario.

   Mario works in a factory. He's worked there for a few months. The factory has a good safety-training program. Every employee is required to take a class and learn about keeping the workplace safe. Mario's co-workers follow the safety rules, but Mario has noticed one unsafe practice at his workplace. Some of the emergency exits are locked, even though a big sign on the door says, "This door must be unlocked at all times during work hours." Mario thinks that the emergency exits should be unlocked, but he doesn't know what to do.

B Work with your classmates. Answer the questions.

1. What is Mario's problem?
2. Give Mario advice. Think of 3 or 4 solutions to his problem.
3. Write Mario a short letter. Tell him what you think he should do.

Getting Ahead

FOCUS ON
- interpersonal skills and personal qualities
- writing a recommendation
- adjective clauses
- asking for information
- building interpersonal skills

LESSON 1 Vocabulary

1 Learn vocabulary for interpersonal skills

A Talk about the questions with your class.

1. What skills do you think help people get better jobs?
2. Which of these skills are also useful at school, at home, and in the community?

B Work with your classmates. Match the words with the pictures.

____ ask for clarification	____ manage conflict	____ solve problems
____ give feedback	____ resolve disagreements	____ work on a team
_1_ make suggestions	____ respond to feedback	

 C Listen and check. Then read the new words with a partner.

D Work with a partner. Write other words that you know for interpersonal skills. Check your words in a dictionary.

✔ Identify and use vocabulary for interpersonal skills and personal qualities

E Work with a partner. Practice the conversation. Use the words in 1B.

A: Do you find it easy to respond to feedback?

B: Pretty easy. How about you?

A: It's not too easy, but I'm working on it.

2 Learn vocabulary to describe personal qualities

A Read the evaluation. Describe Ayana's personal qualities.

Employee Evaluation for: *Ayana Abeb*

Section 1: Personal Qualities

EMPLOYEE IS...	RATING*	COMMENTS
reliable	4	is always on time: completes all work
responsible	4	works well without supervision
flexible	2	sometimes has difficulty making changes
honest	4	reports problems and follows company rules
independent	3	can work alone, but does best work on a team
tolerant	4	works well with everyone: listens to others' ideas

*4= always 3= usually 2= sometimes 1= rarely

B Complete the sentences. Use the words in 2A.

1. Ayana is _reliable_. I know she'll be here every day.

2. You can believe everything she says. She's very _____.

3. She doesn't like to make changes. She needs to be more _____.

4. She's a good team player, but she is also _____.

5. She works hard when the supervisor isn't there. She's _____.

6. She works well with everyone. She's _____.

C Talk about the questions with your class.

1. When you work on a team, which interpersonal skills and personal qualities are the most important? Why?

2. Which skills and qualities are most important in a family? In a class?

TEST YOURSELF ✔

Close your book. Make four lists about your interpersonal skills and personal qualities. *I can... I can't... I am... I'm not...* Check your spelling in a dictionary. Compare your lists with a partner.

1 Read a recommendation

A Look at the *To, From,* and *RE* lines of the memo. Talk about the questions with your class.

1. Do Ms. Roberts and Mr. Scott work at the same company? How do you know?
2. What is the memo about?

B Listen and read the recommendation memo.

> **To:** Annalise Roberts, Human Resources
> **From:** Martin Scott, Accounting
> **RE:** Recommendation for Employee of the Month
>
> I would like to recommend Helen Lee for the Employee of the Month award.
>
> Ms. Lee has been working as a clerk in the accounting department since 2005. She is one of our most reliable and responsible employees. She does her work well and checks it carefully.
>
> Ms. Lee is a good team player. She makes helpful suggestions and often volunteers to stay late when we are especially busy. She gives 110% to make sure that the work gets done.
>
> I hope that you will consider Helen Lee for the Employee of the Month award.

Writer's note

A workplace memo includes *To, From,* and *RE* (subject) lines. Do not indent the paragraphs in a memo or business letter.

C Check your understanding. Complete the sentences with words from 1B.

1. Mr. Scott wrote a __memo__ to Ms. Roberts.
2. Mr. Scott is recommending Ms. Lee for the Employee of the Month _____.
3. Helen Lee is a _____ in the accounting department.
4. Ms. Lee is good at working on a _____.
5. Ms. Lee often makes good _____.
6. When the office is busy, Ms. Lee often _____ to work late.

2 Write a recommendation

A **Talk about the questions with your class.**

1. Imagine you are recommending someone for Employee or Student of the Month. Who would you recommend?
2. Which interpersonal skills and personal qualities does this person have? What does he or she do very well?

B **Write a memo to recommend the person you described in 2A. Use the model in 1B and the questions below to help you.**

To start: What information will you put in the *To, From,* and *RE* lines of your memo?

Paragraph 1: Who do you want to recommend for Employee or Student of the Month?

Paragraph 2: What are this person's special qualities?
What does he or she do very well?
What interpersonal skills does this person have?

To Close: How will you summarize your recommendation?
How will you end your memo?

Need help?

Recommendations
does excellent work
goes beyond the call of duty
gives 110%
goes the extra mile

To:
From:
RE:
I would like to recommend…

C **Use the checklist to edit your writing. Check (✔) the true sentences.**

Editing checklist	
1. I explained what the person does well.	
2. I described the person's personal qualities and interpersonal skills.	
3. My memo includes *To, From,* and *RE* lines.	
4. I grouped my ideas into paragraphs and did not indent them.	

D **Exchange memos with a partner. Read and comment on your partner's work.**

1. Point out the quality or skill you think is most important.
2. Ask a question about the person in your partner's memo.

TEST YOURSELF ✔

Write a new memo or note recommending someone for an award. Write about another person you know who works really hard.

1 Learn adjective clauses

A Read the conversation. Which skill should Alicia work on?

Manager: Here's your evaluation, Alicia. You're doing a great job!

Alicia: Thank you for saying so.

Manager: There's just one skill that needs work. Please try to make better eye contact with the customers who sit at your tables.

Alicia: OK, I will.

B Study the chart. Underline the 2 adjective clauses in the conversation above.

Adjective clauses after main clauses		
Main clause	Adjective clause	
There is one **skill**	which that	needs work.
Please greet the **customers**	who that	sit at your tables.

Notes

• Use adjective clauses to give more information about a noun in the main clause of a sentence:
   Alicia should greet the customers.
   A: Which customers should Alicia greet?
   B: Alicia should greet the customers **who sit at her tables.**
• Use *which* or *that* when the adjective describes a thing.
• Use *who* or *that* when the adjective clause describes a person.

C Combine the sentences with adjective clauses. Use *which* or *who.*

1. The manager made a suggestion. The suggestion helped Alicia.

   The manager made a suggestion which helped Alicia.

2. Alicia has many skills. The skills are important in her job.

   _____

3. She always remembers the customers. The customers sit at her tables.

   _____

4. She is good at solving problems. Problems happen in the kitchen.

   _____

☑ Use adjective clauses to describe job applicants' experience and skills

D **Get the form. Work with your class. Correct the sentences.**

1. Tyra's manager gave her feedback who helped her.

   _____

2. He wants her to manage conflict with the people which work with her.

   _____

3. Tyra is happy to have a new skill who will help her on her team.

   _____

2 Learn adjective clauses inside main clauses

A **Study the chart. Who made a suggestion?**

Adjective clauses inside main clauses			
		Main clause	
	Adjective clause		
The manager	who that	did Alicia's evaluation	made a suggestion.
The company	which that	gave him the job	closed last week.

B **Combine the sentences with adjective clauses. Two answers are possible.**

1. The manager was very happy. He had hired Alicia.

   The manager who had hired Alicia was very happy.
   The manager that had hired Alicia was very happy.

2. The suggestion was about making eye contact. It helped Alicia.

   _____

   _____

3. The job opening was filled last week. It was advertised in the paper.

   _____

   _____

4. The woman quit after two days. She was hired last week.

   _____

   _____

C **Complete the sentences with adjective clauses. Use your own ideas.**

1. A company _____ is a good place to work.
2. People _____ are good employees.
3. A manager _____ is a good person to work for.

3 Grammar listening

A Listen to the conversations. Match the parts of the sentences.

<u>c</u> 1. We're looking for people	a. who work well on a team.
___ 2. We need systems	b. that gets the job must be reliable.
___ 3. She got an evaluation	c. that can manage conflict.
___ 4. We're hiring people	d. who have the right experience.
___ 5. The person	e. that are reliable.
___ 6. We'll interview the applicants	f. which was very positive.

B Listen again and check your answers.

4 Practice adjective clauses

A A hotel has a full-time opening for a front-desk clerk. Look at the list of applicants for the job. How many have hotel experience?

Applicants for Desk Clerk Position:	
Applicant	Notes
1	speaks 5 languages but hasn't worked in a hotel
2	has a lot of experience in hotels in Europe
3	is a housekeeper here now. She's very reliable
4	is currently a desk clerk at a smaller hotel
5	is the hotel owner's nephew but has never had a job
6	has studied hotel management but hasn't worked in a hotel

B Work with a partner. You are managers at the hotel in 4A. Decide which applicant to hire. Give your opinion.

I think we should hire the person who…
The person that… would be better because…

C Tell the class which applicant you have decided to hire and why.

We want to hire the applicant who… because…

> **TEST YOURSELF** ✔
>
> Close your book. Write 5 sentences about your classmates' opinions in 4C.
> Use adjective clauses to write about the job applicant's qualifications.

1 Learn to ask for information

STUDENT AUDIO **A** **Look at the organizational chart. Listen to the conversations. Then answer the questions below with your classmates.**

MARTINEZ ELECTRONICS

George Martinez, General Manager

Marilyn Reese, Warehouse Manager

Gina Anderson, Human Resources Supervisor

Martin Gupta, Benefits Officer

Teresa Bell, Payroll Clerk   **Jun Kim,** Payroll Clerk

1. Who should Marta see about her schedule?
2. Who should Jamal talk to about the memo that he received?

STUDENT AUDIO **B** **Listen and read. Why shouldn't the employee talk to her manager first?**

A: Hey! You look upset. What's wrong?

B: There's a problem with my paycheck.
   Who should I see about it?

A: Go see Ms. Bell.

B: Ms. Bell? Who's she?

A: You know. She's the woman whose office is next to the time clock.

B: Should I talk to my manager first?

A: Uh-uh. You should go directly to Ms. Bell.
   She's the person who takes care of payroll problems. That's the procedure here.

B: OK, thanks. I'll see you later.

> **In other words...**
>
> **Asking for information**
> Who should I see about...?
> Who do I talk to?
> What should I do?
> What do I do about...?

C **Role-play a conversation with a partner about asking for information. Use the example in 1B to make a new conversation.**

Partner A: You're a student and there's a problem with your class schedule. Ask your classmate who you should see about it. Ask if you should talk to your teacher first. Thank your classmate for helping you.

Partner B: You're a student. Your classmate asks you a question. Tell your classmate to see Mr. Ang, the coordinator. His office is downstairs. He takes care of schedule problems.

2 Learn adjective clauses with *whose*

A Study the chart. Who are Mr. and Mrs. Lopez?

Adjective clauses with *whose*	
Main clause	Adjective clause
Ms. Bell is the **clerk**	**whose office** is next to the time clock.
Mr. and Mrs. Lopez are the **people**	**whose children** won awards.

Note
Adjective clauses with *whose* show who something belongs to.

B Work with a partner. Combine the sentences with *whose*. Then use the new sentence in a conversation.

1. Margaret is one of the cashiers. Her schedule is the same as Tom's.
   A: *Who is Margaret?*
   B: *She's the cashier whose schedule is the same as Tom's.*
2. Mr. Edwards is one of the teachers. His office is on the second floor.
3. Natasha and Jim are the employees. Their paychecks were lost.
4. Sophie is one of the managers. Her office is down the hall.

C Work with a partner. Complete the sentences with adjective clauses.

1. Mr. Kelso is the teacher <u>whose class meets at three o'clock</u>.
2. Terry is the manager _____.
3. Daria is the woman _____.
4. Mr. and Mrs. Silva are the people _____.

3 Practice your pronunciation

A Listen to the conversations. Notice how the speakers say *Yes* and *No*. Practice the conversations with a partner.

1. A: Do I talk to my manager first?
   B: Uh-uh. You go to Ms. Bell.

2. A: Does Mr. Sosa work here?
   B: Uh-huh. Do you need to talk to him?

   Note: Do not use *Uh-uh* or *Uh-huh* in formal situations.

B Work with a partner. Ask and answer the questions. Use *Uh-huh* and *Uh-uh* to say *Yes* or *No*. Then add more information, as in 1A.

1. Do you work in an office?
2. Were you in class yesterday?
3. Have you ever gotten an award?
4. Do you like to work on a team?

4 Focus on listening

A **Talk about the questions with your class.**

1. What are some reasons employees call a company?

2. What are some reasons customers call a company?

B **Listen to the automated phone menu. Number the offices in the order you hear them.**

_____ Business Services	_____ Main Office
_____ Customer Service	__1__ Sales and Service
_____ Human Resources	_____ Warehouse

C **Listen again. Complete the phone directory for Martinez Electronics.**

Office	Extension
Business Services	
Customer Service	
Human Resources	
Main Office	
Sales and Service	111
Warehouse	

5 Real-life math

A **Read the problem and answer the question.**

Martinez Electronics		Name: Tom Tran		Check # 3133	
Gross Pay	Social Security	Medicare	Federal Tax	State Tax	Net Pay
$421.40	$26.13	$6.11	$11.03	$13.80	**$355.36**

Tom called Ms. Bell in Payroll because he thinks there is an error on his paycheck. He thinks his net pay is incorrect. What should Tom's net pay be? _____

B **Explain your answer to your classmates.**

TEST YOURSELF ✔

Role-play a conversation between two neighbors. Partner A: Something in your apartment isn't working. Ask your partner who to call. You think you should call the repairperson. Partner B: Tell your neighbor that he or she needs to call the apartment manager first. Then change roles.

1 Get ready to read

A What do you think *people skills* are? Give some examples.

B Read the definitions. What are you enthusiastic about?

diverse: (adj.) including a lot of differences
enthusiastic: (adj.) excited, very positive
pay off: (verb) to produce a benefit

C Read the questions in 2C on page 85. Look for the answers as you read the article in 2A.

2 Read and respond

A Read the article. Did the students enjoy the training class?

Skills Training Pays Off for Local Residents

Last Thursday, the Pasco Adult Skills Program celebrated the end of its spring semester with a party for graduates of its 12-week *People Skills* training class. The graduates were enthusiastic about the program and its results.

"I learned about teamwork," said Daniela Victor, age 27. "Before I took this class, I thought that people who worked in groups could never get anything done. Now I know that when people work together, they get a lot more work done. I'm a more tolerant and more flexible person now.

"I really appreciated the emphasis[1] on language," said Musa Tahri, 45. "I needed to learn the right English to work in a group and manage conflict. Everything we did in class is paying off. The skills I learned are helping me at work, in my community, and even at home. I'm helping my kids learn to resolve disagreements and find solutions to problems by talking. Those skills are helping them in school, too!"

A third graduate, Diego Rosario, 66, was also enthusiastic. "I'm so glad I came here," said Rosario. "I've met men and women from all over the world, and I've learned a lot about working with diverse groups of people. I'm using the skills I learned to start a community parks group in my neighborhood."

Pasco Adult School's next *People Skills* training class is scheduled to begin in September. For more information, call (250) 555-1800.

[1]emphasis: a strong focus on something

☑ Use previewing strategies to better understand a reading passage

B Listen and read the article again.

C Work with a partner. Ask and answer the questions.

1. What class did the three students take?
2. What does Daniela Victor think now about people who work together?
3. What personal qualities did Daniela Victor develop in the class?
4. How is Musa Tahri using his new skills?

D Study the chart. Circle the correct words in the sentences below.

Word Study: The prefixes *dis-*, *in-*, and *un-*

Add *dis-*, *in-*, *ir-*, and *un-* to the beginning of some adjectives to form negatives.

Adjective	Negative	Adjective	Negative
responsible	irresponsible	reliable	unreliable
flexible	inflexible	honest	dishonest

---

1. Some of my co-workers come late and are very (dependable / unreliable), but Laura is (responsible / irresponsible) and always finishes her work on time.

2. Edward is (flexible / inflexible); he can't make changes. And sometimes he's (honest / dishonest) and breaks the company rules. The company shouldn't hire someone who's this (reliable / irresponsible).

3 Talk it over

Think about the questions. Talk about your ideas with the class.

1. Many people say that it's important to be able to work with diverse groups of people. Do you agree? Why or why not?
2. What are some things that help people in diverse groups work together?
3. How can you have good interpersonal skills in a language you don't know well?

BRING IT TO LIFE

Use the newspaper, a magazine, or the Internet to find an article or cartoon about interpersonal skills in the workplace. Bring it to class and talk about it with your classmates.

---

1 Grammar

A Circle the correct words.

1. The company ((that) / who) makes these boxes is in our town.
2. The people (which / who) work there say that it's a good company.
3. I know several people (who / whose) parents worked there.
4. The owner of the company is the person (that / which) hired me.
5. A lot of companies use the boxes (which / who) are made here.
6. The employees (who / whose) work is the best get awards every year.

B Match the parts of the sentences.

_c_	1. The manager	a.	whose benefits were increased was very happy.
____	2. The employee	b.	which require experience are harder to get.
____	3. Employees	c.	that prepared the report did a good job.
____	4. Jobs	d.	who are honest are very valuable.

C Combine the sentences. Use adjective clauses with *who, that,* or *which*.

1. I like working with people. People can resolve disagreements.

   <u>I like working with people who can resolve disagreements.</u>

2. Disagreements can cause big problems on the job. The disagreements aren't resolved.

   _____

3. The manager gives a lot of feedback. She hired me.

   _____

4. The team won $100. The team solved the problem.

   _____

D Combine the sentences. Use adjective clauses with *whose*.

1. Ms. Haines is the teacher. Her class always has the most students.

   <u>Ms. Haines is the teacher whose class always has the most students.</u>

2. Mr. Freeman is the art teacher. His students painted these pictures.

   _____

3. Mr. Diaz was the counselor. His suggestions really helped me.

   _____

4. Mrs. Tanaka was the principal. Her office was very nice.

   _____

2 Group work

 A Work with 2–3 classmates. Write a 6–8 line conversation between the people in the picture. Share your conversation with the class.

A: *Let's take a look at your evaluation.*
B: *OK.*
A: *First, you're doing a good job at...*

B Interview 3 classmates. Write their answers.

1. Do you know someone who gets along with everyone? Who is it? How does he/she do it?
2. Which interpersonal skill would you like to develop? Why?
3. What are three things that every manager (or teacher or parent) should do? Why?

C Talk about your answers with your class.

PROBLEM SOLVING

 A Listen and read about Lana.

Lana has just gotten a promotion at work. She is a team manager for a group of six employees. Lana really wants to be a success in her new job, but her group isn't really a team. Two of the people in her group don't like each other and argue a lot. There is one team member who talks all the time and another one who never says a word. The team members are from six different countries, and two of the countries they come from don't get along. Lana doesn't know what to do.

B Work with your classmates. Answer the questions.

1. What is Lana's problem?
2. What should she do? Think of 2 or 3 solutions to her problem.
3. Write a short letter to Lana. Tell her what you think she should do.

Buy Now, Pay Later

FOCUS ON
• personal finance and budgeting
• essay writing
• present unreal conditionals
• negotiating and compromising
• financial planning

LESSON 1 Vocabulary

1 Learn vocabulary for personal finance and banking

A **Talk about the questions with your class.**

1. What are some services that banks and credit unions offer?
2. Are you good at managing money? What money skills do you have?

B **Work with your classmates. Match the words with the picture.**

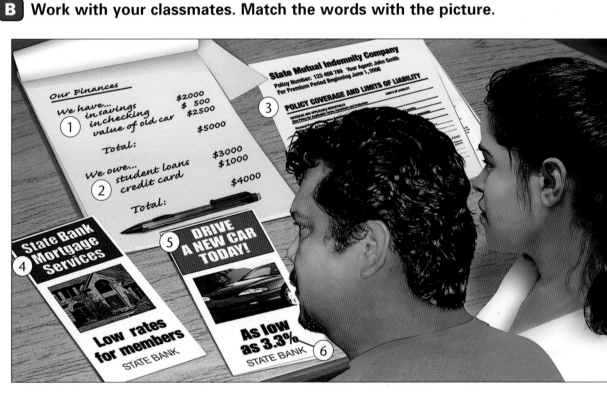

__1__ assets	____ debts	____ insurance policy
____ auto loan	____ home loan	____ interest rate

C **Listen and check. Then read the new words with a partner.**

D **Work with a partner. Write other personal finance and banking words you know. Check your words in a dictionary.**

☑ Identify and use financial and banking vocabulary to discuss budgeting

E **Work with a partner. Talk about the questions. Use the words in 1B.**

1. What types of accounts and loans do banks offer?
2. What types of assets and debts do people often have?
3. What kinds of insurance do people often have?

2 Learn budgeting vocabulary

A **Look at Julia and Roberto's budget. Match the words with their definitions.**

Our budget: Sanchez-Ruiz family

Net Income	Julia's job		$1200 per month
	Roberto's job		$1200 per month
Expenses	Fixed Expenses	Rent	$900 per month
		Car insurance premium	$200 per month
	Variable Expenses	food	$400 per month
		utilities	$200 per month
		car (gas)	$300 per month
		miscellaneous (clothing, gifts, eating out, etc.)	$400 per month

Mortgage payment for house= $1,035 per month

_d_ 1. fixed expenses   a. money from a job or other sources

____ 2. variable expenses   b. money you pay for insurance

____ 3. income   c. things that cost a different amount each month

____ 4. mortgage payment   d. things that cost the same each month

____ 5. premium   e. things that don't fit in any other category

____ 6. miscellaneous   f. money you pay for a home loan

B **Work with a partner. Practice the conversation. Use the words and amounts in 2A.**

A: How much did we pay for utilities last month?

B: Look under variable expenses.

A: We paid $200! Wow! I didn't know it was that much.

C **Talk about the questions with your class.**

1. How does making a budget help a family?
2. Julia and Roberto want to save for a house. What advice can you give them?

TEST YOURSELF ✔

Close your book. Work with a partner. Make a list of as many new words from the lesson as you can. Alphabetize your list. Check your spelling in a dictionary.

1 Read an essay about money

A Talk about the questions with your class.

1. What are some ways that having or not having money affects people's lives?
2. In your opinion, do people pay too much attention to money? Explain your answer.

B Listen and read the essay about money.

Topic
Tell why you agree or disagree with this statement:
"Money can't buy happiness." Limit your essay to 125 words.

Money Can't Buy Happiness
by Edwin Thomas

Money is important. People who have money have more comfortable lives than people who don't have money. They have more free time, more security, and more flexibility.

Most people would probably say that they would like to have more money. However, many of these people would probably also agree that money can't buy happiness.

Happiness is a feeling. It can come from being with your family or your friends, from good news, from kind words, or from a happy event. Money can help make good things happen, but it can't buy time, friends, or love. Money can only buy things.

People can find happiness in everyday life and in other people. Sometimes money can help, but the statement is still true: "Money can't buy happiness."

Writer's note

Formal essays don't usually use the first-person pronoun *I* or statements like *I think*...or *In my opinion*.

C Check your understanding. Answer the questions.

1. According to Edwin, what 4 things can money buy?
   comfortable lives, free time, security, and flexibility

2. What does he think most people want? _____

3. According to Edwin, what things bring happiness? _____

4. Does Edwin agree or disagree with the statement "Money can't buy happiness"?

   _____

2 Write an essay about money

 A **Talk about the questions with your class.**

1. Name three famous people who have a lot of money. What do you think their lives are like?
2. What have these three people done to change the world or to help others?
3. Name someone who has changed the world. Did the person use money to make changes?

B **Write an essay about money. Read the directions. Use the model in 1B and the questions below to help you.**

> **Topic**
> Tell why you agree or disagree with this statement: "Money makes the world go around." Limit your essay to 125 words.

Paragraph 1: How does money change the world? What would most people probably say that money can do?

Paragraph 2: What are some things in the world that money cannot change?

Paragraph 3: Is it true that money makes the world go around? If not, what "makes the world go around"?

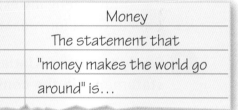

Money

The statement that

"money makes the world go

around" is...

C **Use the checklist to edit your writing. Check (✔) the true sentences.**

Editing checklist	
1. I wrote about the topic in the directions.	
2. I gave my opinions without using *I*.	
3. I used commas between items in lists.	
4. My essay is not more than 125 words.	

D **Exchange essays with a partner. Read and comment on your partner's work.**

1. Point out one sentence you think is interesting.
2. Ask a question about one idea in your partner's essay.

TEST YOURSELF ✔

Think about a popular saying about money in your first language. Translate the saying and write a new essay that explains why you agree or disagree with the saying.

1 Learn present unreal conditional statements

A **Read the conversation. Can Molly go to college right now? Why or why not?**

Isabel: If I go to the cafe for lunch, will you go with me?

Molly: Thanks, but I don't think so. I brought a sandwich from home. I'm really trying to save money.

Isabel: I know. If I didn't eat in the cafe every day, I'd save about $25 a week.

Molly: I'm saving for college—that's my dream. If I had enough money, I'd start today. But I don't, so I'm watching my expenses.

Isabel: Good for you, Molly! Go get your dream.

B **Study the chart. Underline the 2 examples of present unreal conditional statements in the conversation above.**

Present unreal conditional statements	
If clause	Main clause
If Molly **had** enough money,	she **could start** college now.
If she **had** enough money now,	she **wouldn't have to wait**.
If Isabel **didn't eat** in the cafe,	she **would save** money.

Notes

• Use unreal conditional statements to talk about unreal, untrue, or impossible situations:
  If Molly had enough money, she could start college now.
  (She doesn't have enough money. She can't start college now.)
• In unreal conditionals, the *if* clause can also come after the main clause:
  Molly could start college now **if she had enough money**.

C **Complete the sentences to make present unreal conditional statements. Use the verbs in parentheses.**

1. It ____would be____ easier for Isabel to save money if she ____limited____ her spending. (be, limit)

2. If she _____ the bus, she _____ a lot of money on parking. (take, save)

3. If she _____ Town Bank, she _____ a higher interest rate. (use, get)

4. Isabel _____ $100 a month if she _____ her lunch. (save, bring)

D Get the form. Work with your class. Correct the sentences.

1. Sunny would spend less money if she shops at garage sales. _____
2. If she did that, she will also meet her neighbors. _____
3. She can start this weekend if she wanted to. _____

2 Learn present unreal conditional questions

A Study the charts. Circle the correct words in the questions below.

Yes/No questions and short answers
A: **Would** Molly **go** to college **if** she **didn't have to work**? B: Yes, she **would**.
A: **If** your son **wanted** a credit card, **would** you **give** him one? B: No, I **wouldn't**.

Information questions
A: What **would** Molly **do** if she **had** enough money? B: She **would go** to college.
A: **If** you **could live** anywhere, where **would** you **live**? B: I **would live** in Hawaii.

Note
Don't use contracted forms (*she'd, he'd,* etc.) in affirmative short answers.

1. Who would you call if you (have / had) a money emergency?
2. Would he save a lot of money if he (walked / would walk) to work?

B Complete the questions and answers. Use the verbs in parentheses.

1. A: If you ___*didn't need*___ money, ___*would*___ you ___*keep*___ your second job? (not need, keep)

   B: Yes, I ___*would*___. I like that job.

2. A: If you _____ a car, _____ you _____ to work? (have, drive)

   B: No, I _____. Gas is too expensive.

3. A: How much money _____ she _____ if she _____ at expensive stores? (save, not shop)

   B: She _____ fifty or sixty dollars a month. (save)

4. A: What _____ you _____ first if you _____ to buy a house? (do, want)

   B: I _____ some information on home loans. (get)

3 Grammar listening

Listen to the conversations. Check (✔) the true sentences.

1. _____   a. She has a credit card.
   _✔_   b. She has to carry cash.
2. _____   a. He uses a credit card.
   _____   b. He doesn't use a credit card.
3. _____   a. She has to study.
   _____   b. She rents a movie every night.
4. _____   a. He has to study.
   _____   b. He would like to rent a movie every night.

4 Practice present unreal conditionals

A Think about your answers to these questions.

1. If you had $100 to spend on your classroom or school, how would you spend the money? Why?
2. What would you do if you had $1,000 to spend on your classroom or school? Why?
3. If you could make one change in your school, what would you change?

B Work with a partner. Ask and answer the questions in 4A.

A: *If you had $100 to spend on our classroom, how would you spend the money?*
B: *I would buy a dictionary for every student.*
A: *Why would you do that?*
B: *Well, I'd do it because…*

C Talk about your ideas with the class. Which ideas do you like best?

If we had $100 to spend on our classroom, we would…

TEST YOURSELF ✔

Close your book. Write 5 sentences about how you and your classmates would spend money on your classroom or school. Use present unreal conditionals.

1 Learn to negotiate and compromise on a budget

STUDENT AUDIO 🎧 **A** **Look at the picture. Listen to the conversation. Then answer the questions below with your classmates.**

1. How much do Julia and Roberto agree to spend on food?
2. How much do they agree to spend on entertainment?

STUDENT AUDIO 🎧 **B** **Listen and read. What do Julia and Roberto decide?**

Julia: You know, if you didn't buy coffee on the way to work, we'd save a lot of money.

Roberto: You mean quit drinking coffee?

Julia: No, but those coffee places are expensive.

Roberto: What if I made coffee at home and took it to work? And how about if you stopped buying snacks at work?

Julia: Let's compromise. I'll bring my own snacks...

Roberto: ...And I'll make my own coffee. And we'll save about $100 a month.

Julia: It's a deal!*

***Idiom note:** It's a deal = I agree; let's do it

> **In other words...**
>
> **Making suggestions**
> What if I/you +
>   (simple past verb)...?
> How about if I/you +
>   (simple past verb)...?
> How about ...?
> Let's make it ....

C **Role-play a compromise with a partner. Use the example in 1B to make a new conversation.**

Partner A: You and your roommate want to save money. Suggest that if your roommate stopped buying fresh fruit at Helson's, you'd save a lot of money. Explain that Helson's is an expensive grocery store. Offer a compromise. You'll buy fewer microwave meals and do more cooking. Agree with your roommate.

Partner B: Check to see if your roommate wants you to stop buying fresh fruit. Offer to buy fruit on sale and suggest that your roommate stop buying so many expensive microwave meals. Come to an agreement.

☑ Ask and answer questions about expenses in order to plan a budget   **95**

2 Learn present unreal conditionals with *be*

A Look at the picture in the chart. Is Jason's father giving him good advice?

Present unreal conditionals with *be*

What would you do?

If I were you, I'd look for a newer car.

$2,000
1998

If his father weren't here, Jason would buy the car.

Note

In formal speech with present unreal conditionals, use *were* for all people (*I, you, he, she*, etc.).
If I **were** you, I'd look for a newer car.

B Work with a partner. Use the words below and your own ideas to make a conversation.

1. the owner of a big company

   A: *What would you do if you were the owner of a big company?*
   B: *If I were the owner of a big company, I would…*

2. a millionaire

3. the president of the United States

4. the director of this school

3 Practice your pronunciation

A Listen to the sentences. Notice that the speakers pause at the commas.

1. If I were you, I wouldn't buy that car.

2. If you had the money, a newer car would probably be better.

B Circle the commas in these sentences. Say the sentences. Then listen and check the pauses.

1. If I were Jason, I'd keep looking.
2. That car is old, but it runs well.
3. If you bought an older car, it'd cost less.
4. If he bought a new car, he'd be in debt.
5. If he buys this car, he won't be in debt.
6. He can take a bus, so a car isn't necessary.

C Practice the sentences in 3A and 3B with a partner.

4 Focus on listening

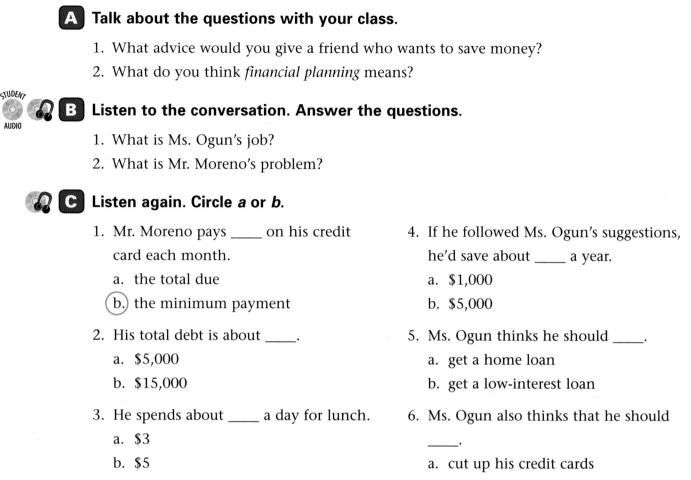

A **Talk about the questions with your class.**

1. What advice would you give a friend who wants to save money?
2. What do you think *financial planning* means?

B **Listen to the conversation. Answer the questions.**

1. What is Ms. Ogun's job?
2. What is Mr. Moreno's problem?

C **Listen again. Circle *a* or *b*.**

1. Mr. Moreno pays _____ on his credit card each month.
   a. the total due
   b. the minimum payment

2. His total debt is about _____.
   a. $5,000
   b. $15,000

3. He spends about _____ a day for lunch.
   a. $3
   b. $5

4. If he followed Ms. Ogun's suggestions, he'd save about _____ a year.
   a. $1,000
   b. $5,000

5. Ms. Ogun thinks he should _____.
   a. get a home loan
   b. get a low-interest loan

6. Ms. Ogun also thinks that he should _____.
   a. cut up his credit cards
   b. put his cards away for one year

5 Real-life math

A **Read the story and answer the question.**

Veronica's paycheck is $1,050 a month after deductions. She pays $450 a month for rent, $75 a month for utilities, and $45 a month for health insurance. If she put $90 a month into a savings account, how much would she have left for other expenses? _____

B **Explain your answer to your classmates.**

> **TEST YOURSELF** ✔
>
> Role-play a conversation between co-workers planning a party at work. Partner A: You want each employee to give $20 for food and drinks. Partner B: You think $20 is too much. You think it would be better if everyone brought food. Compromise and make a plan with your co-worker. Then change roles.

1 Get ready to read

 A **Why is it important to save money for the future? Is it easy to save? Why or why not?**

B **Read the definitions. Which word means *suggest*?**

advise: (verb) to give advice, make a suggestion
equivalent: (noun) an equal amount
intimidating: (adj.) frightening, scary

C **Look at the title, the chart, and the headings in the article in 2A. What do you think the article is about?**

2 Read and respond

A **Read the article. Who do you think this advice is good for?**

SAVING: THE KEY TO REACHING YOUR GOALS

BY CECILIA OGUN

FINANCIAL PLANNING

Do you remember your grandmother talking about "saving for a rainy day?" My grandmother knew how important it was to have savings. If she were here today, she'd be a financial planner!

Financial planning means deciding how you want to use your money. It's important in today's economy, and it's the best way to afford "big-ticket" items, like a new home, a car, college tuition, and retirement.

MAKING A PLAN

Financial planning may sound intimidating, but it isn't. The first step is to make a record of your income and expenses. As a financial planner, I advise keeping track of all your expenditures[1] for a month, to see where the money is going. Next, I tell my clients to decide how much they can afford to put into savings each month. I recommend saving 10 percent of your take-home pay. One common method is to "pay" yourself first by putting money into savings as soon as you get a paycheck.

[1]expenditures: expenses, costs

HOW SAVINGS GROW

If you saved a dollar a day in a jar in your kitchen, you would have $365 in savings by the end of a year. If you saved the same money in the bank at four percent interest, you'd have $372 at the end of a year. The chart shows the difference over 30 years; it really adds up!

$1 a day for:	equals:	with 4% daily interest, it's:
1 year	$ 365	$ 372
5 years	$ 1,825	$ 2,929
10 years	$ 3,650	$ 4,487
30 years	$ 10,950	$ 21,169

SAVING FOR A RAINY DAY

Emergencies are the "rainy days" we hope will never come. It's a good idea to keep the equivalent of three to six months' living expenses in a savings account, in case of an emergency.

Planning and saving are the keys to a healthy financial future, and they are available to everyone. So take Grandma's advice, and start your savings plan today.

Source: www.pueblo.gsa.gov

B **Listen and read the article again.**

C **Complete the sentences with words from the article.**

1. In today's _____ economy _____, it's important to have a financial plan.

2. _____ items are expensive things that might require a loan. Two examples are _____ and _____.

3. Ms. Ogun recommends putting 10 percent of your _____ into savings.

4. It's a good idea to save money in a bank because it will earn _____.

5. Ms. Ogun's advice is to have enough money for three to six months' _____ in savings.

3 Talk it over

Think about the questions. Talk about your ideas with the class.

1. How did you learn about spending and saving money when you were a child? Who do you think should teach children about money?

2. How have your feelings about money changed over the last ten years?

BRING IT TO LIFE

Use the newspaper, a magazine, or the Internet to find an article on ways to save money. Talk about your article with your classmates.

1 Grammar

A **Read the information. Which statements are true? Circle *a* or *b*.**

1. Ed would buy a car if he didn't have credit card debts.
    a. Ed has credit card debts.
    b. Ed doesn't have credit card debts.

2. If Joan had to pay for her checks, she would change banks.
    a. Joan has to pay for her checks.
    b. Joan doesn't have to pay for her checks.

3. If you didn't have an ATM card, you'd have to write a check to get cash.
    a. You have an ATM card.
    b. You have to write a check to get cash.

B **Complete the sentences to make present unreal conditional statements. Use the verbs in parentheses.**

1. If we _saved_ a little every month, we _would have_ money for emergencies. (save, have)
2. We _____ fewer disagreements if we _____ more about spending. (have, talk)
3. We _____ checks if we _____ our bills online. (not have to write, pay)
4. If I always _____ the checkbook in the desk, it _____ easier to find it. (put, be)

C **Complete the questions and answers with present unreal conditionals. Use the words in parentheses.**

1. A: If _____I kept_____ (I/keep) a list of everything I spend, _would you do_ (you/do) it, too?

    B: Yes, I _____would_____.

2. A: _____ (you/be) unhappy if _____ (we/spend) less on travel?

    B: No, I _____. That's fine with me.

3. A: How _____ (you/cut) your expenses if _____ (you/want) to save money?

    B: _____ (I/not buy) things if _____ (I not need) them.

4. A: What _____ (you/do) if _____ (you/be) in debt?

    B: I _____ (get) a second job.

2 Group work

A Work with 2–3 classmates. Write a 6–8 line conversation between the people in the picture. Share your conversation with the class.

A: *What is your financial goal for the future?*
   What would you like to do?
B: *Well, I'd like to…*
A: *OK. If I were you,…*

B Interview 3 classmates. Write their answers.

1. Are you a spender or a saver?
2. What do you think is the best way to save money?
3. If you could give everyone in this class one piece of advice about money, what would it be?

C Talk about the answers with your class.

PROBLEM SOLVING

A Listen and read about Lula.

   Lula's best friend, Adele, has a money problem. Adele has a good job and she makes a good salary, but she isn't very careful with her money. For example, she likes nice clothes, and she often buys them. She always has lunch at a restaurant on workdays, and she eats dinner out several nights a week, too. When she buys groceries, she shops at an expensive supermarket because the food looks so good there. Adele is a generous person, and she often buys expensive gifts for her friends. Lula doesn't think Adele puts any money into savings, and she's worried about her. What should Lula do?

B Work with your classmates. Answer the questions.

1. What is Lula's problem?
2. What would you do if you were Lula? Think of 2 or 3 solutions to her problem.
3. Write a short letter to Lula. Tell her what you think she should do.

UNIT 8

Satisfaction Guaranteed

FOCUS ON
- shopping and purchase problems
- problems with an order
- adjectives and adverbs of degree
- ordering by phone
- consumer protection

LESSON 1 Vocabulary

1 Learn shopping vocabulary

A **Talk about the questions with your class.**

1. Where do you like to shop for the things you need? Why?
2. Have you ever bought something without going to a store?
   If so, what did you buy and how did you buy it?

B **Work with your classmates. Match the words with the pictures.**

_____	as is	_____	on clearance	_____	thrift store
_____	catalog	_____	online store	_____	TV shopping network
_____	flea market	_1_	on sale	_____	yard sale

C **Listen and check. Then read the new words with a partner.**

D **Work with a partner. Write other shopping words you know.**
Check your words in a dictionary.

---

102 ☑ Identify and use shopping vocabulary; describe problems with a purchase

E Work with a partner. Talk about the questions. Use the words in 1B.

1. How do you like to shop? Why?
2. Which kinds of shopping have you never tried? Why or why not?
3. How can you get the best prices on clothes and household items? Explain.

2 Learn to describe purchase problems

A Look at the picture. Complete the customers' sentences below.

RETURNS AND DEFECTIVE MERCHANDISE

SCRATCHED   FADED   DENTED   STAINED   TORN   DEFECTIVE

OUR GUARANTEE:

FULL REFUND ON ANY PURCHASE WITHIN 30 DAYS

Doesn't work

1. "One part of it is a lighter color. It's _____ faded _____."
2. "The glass has a big mark on it. It's _____."
3. "It's new, but it doesn't work. It's _____."
4. "I think something hit it. It's _____."
5. "This happened the first time I put it on. It's _____."
6. "It looks like there's coffee on it. It's _____."

B Work with a partner. Practice the conversation. Use the words in 2A.

A: Excuse me. I'd like to return this mirror. It's scratched.
B: Certainly. We can give you a refund.
A: On second thought, could I exchange it for another one?
B: Of course.

C Talk about the questions with your class.

1. Which items are best to buy in person? By mail? Over the phone? On the Internet? Why?
2. What are some possible problems with items you buy at yard sales, flea markets, or thrift stores? What can you do about these problems?

TEST YOURSELF ✔

Close your book. Categorize the new words in three lists: *Ways to Shop, Sale Descriptions,* and *Reasons for Returns.* Check your spelling in a dictionary. Compare your lists with a partner.

1 Read an email about problems with an order

A **Talk about the questions with your class.**

1. Have you ever written an email about a problem with an item? If so, what did you say? What happened?
2. Look at the email in 1B. Who wrote the email? Who did she write to?

B **Listen and read the email.**

Writer's note

Use words like *first, second,* and *finally* to help the reader identify the important parts of your message.

⊠ **Email - Message (Plain Text)** _ □ x

File   Edit   View   Insert   Format   Tools   Actions   Help

Reply │ Reply to All │ Forward │ Print │ Save │ Delete │ Previous

From: btate@tates.us
To: Customerservice@kitchenetix.corp
Subject: Problems with order #06201

I ordered a coffee maker (item #18834) from your website two weeks ago. It came yesterday, and I was very disappointed. It's not what I ordered.

First, in the picture on your website, the coffee maker is white, but you sent me a black one. Second, there is a problem with the cord. The electric plug is defective. Finally, it said on your website that I would receive two free coffee cups if I ordered by May 31, but the cups were not in the box.

I would like to exchange the black coffee maker for a white one. I would also like to get the free coffee cups. Please reply by email and let me know how to exchange the coffee maker.

Thank you,
Bonnie Tate

C **Check your understanding. Work with a partner. Ask and answer the questions.**

1. Why did Bonnie Tate write the order number in the subject line?
2. What information did she give in the first sentence of her email? Why?
3. How many problems did she write about? How did she organize the information?
4. What does Bonnie want?

2 Write an email about problems with an order

A **Talk about the questions with your class.**

1. Have you ever had problems with things that you have bought? If so, what were the problems? What did you do?

2. What information is important to include in a letter or an email about an item that is defective or incorrect?

B **Write an email about one of the problems you described in 2A. Use the model in 1B and the questions below to help you.**

To start: What is the email address of the company you are writing to?
What is the subject of your email?

Paragraph 1: What did you buy? When did you get it?

Paragraph 2: What were the problems with the item?

Paragraph 3: What would you like the company to do?
How can they contact you?

From:
To:
Subject:
I ordered...

C **Use the checklist to edit your writing. Check (✔) the true sentences.**

Editing checklist	
1. I included information that identifies the product.	
2. I explained the problems clearly.	
3. I used *first, second,* and *finally* to organize my ideas.	
4. I told the company what I want and how to contact me.	

D **Exchange emails with a partner. Read and comment on your partner's work.**

1. Ask a question about the problem in your partner's email.
2. Do you think the company will do what your partner is asking? Why or why not?

TEST YOURSELF ✔

Write a new email about a real or imaginary problem with a purchase you recently made.

1 Learn adjectives ending in -ed and -ing

A **Read the conversation. Does Cho like or dislike the video game? Why?**

Cho: I bought this new video game, and I'm really disappointed with it.

Todd: You are? Why?

Cho: Well, it was supposed to be exciting, but it's not. It's boring.

Todd: Can you return it?

Cho: Just because I don't like it? I don't think so. If you're interested in it, you can have it.

Todd: Uh...OK, thanks.

B **Study the chart. Circle the 2 examples of adjectives ending in -ing and the 2 adjectives ending in -ed in the conversation above.**

Adjectives ending in -ed and -ing	
Adjectives ending in -ed	Adjectives ending in -ing
Cho was **disappointed** with the game.	The game was **disappointing**.
We were **bored** with the movie. We left after 15 minutes.	The movie was really **boring**.

Notes
• Adjectives ending in -ed describe a person's feelings: Cho was **disappointed** because the game wasn't good.
• Adjectives ending in -ing describe the cause of the feelings: Cho was unhappy because the game wasn't **exciting**.

C **Circle the correct adjective.**

1. We were really (boring / (bored)) last night, so we rented a movie and ordered a pizza.

2. The pizza wasn't very good. I was (disappointing / disappointed).

3. The movie was (confusing / confused) at first. I couldn't understand it.

4. After about 30 minutes, though, the movie got much more (exciting / excited).

5. The ending was great. It was really (surprising / surprised).

6. Are you (interesting / interested) in seeing the movie? I think you'd like it.

7. My husband and I are usually too (tiring / tired) to watch movies at night.

8. But that movie sounds (exciting / excited), so maybe we'll rent it on Saturday.

D **Get the meaning. Work with your class. Which statements are true? Circle *a* or *b*.**

1. Sam didn't like his old video games. Nothing happened in the old games.
   a. Sam was bored by the games.
   b. Sam was boring.

2. Some of the new games are difficult to play. Sam doesn't understand them.
   a. The games are confusing.
   b. Sam is confusing.

3. Sam loves the newest video game. It has lots of dangerous adventures.
   a. The new game is excited.
   b. Sam is excited.

2 Learn adverbs of degree

A **Study the chart. Circle the correct adverbs in the sentences below.**

Adverbs of degree			
I'm **a little** confused. I'm **somewhat** confused.	I'm **pretty** confused. I'm **fairly** confused.	I'm **really** confused! I'm **very** confused!	I'm **extremely** confused!

1. The customer said he was never coming back. He was ((really) / a little) annoyed.
2. Don't throw your receipts away! It's (extremely / fairly) important to keep them.
3. I got this book on sale for 90% off, so it was (very / fairly) cheap.
4. The watch is in good condition. It's only (a little / extremely) scratched.

B **Complete the sentences with an adverb of degree or the word *not*. Compare your ideas with a partner.**

1. I am _____ comfortable with shopping in stores in the U.S.
2. Returning items to the store is _____ easy for me.
3. Return policies and guarantees are _____ difficult for me to understand.
4. Ordering items from a catalog is _____ easy for me.
5. Shopping at yard sales and flea markets is _____ unusual for me.

3 Grammar listening

Listen to the sentences. Circle *a* or *b*.

1. a. Actually, it was a little disappointing.
   b. Actually, it was a little disappointed.

2. a. Not really. I was pretty confused at first.
   b. Not really. I was pretty confusing at first.

3. a. I thought it was a little bored.
   b. I thought it was a little boring.

4. a. They thought I was excited.
   b. They thought it was exciting.

5. a. No, I didn't. That's surprising.
   b. No, I didn't. He's surprising.

6. a. No, thanks. I'm really not interesting.
   b. No, thanks. I'm really not interested.

4 Practice adjectives ending in *-ed/-ing* and adverbs of degree

A Think about each of the experiences below.

1. a time when you did something really exciting
2. a time when you did something really interesting
3. a time when you were really bored
4. a time when you were really confused

B Work with a group. Describe one or more of the experiences from 4A.

I did something really exciting when I was 15. I…

C Talk about your experiences with your classmates.

Angela did something really exciting when she was 15. She…

TEST YOURSELF ✔

Close your book. Write 5 sentences about your experiences and about the experiences of the people in your group. Use -ed/-ing adjectives and adverbs of degree:
Klaus was really bored when…

1 Learn to place a catalog order by phone

STUDENT AUDIO **A** Look at the catalog page. Listen to the conversations. Does the customer order the backpack in conversation 1? In conversation 2?

BACKPACKS

The Campus Pack 600

Holds a laptop computer!
Available in blue.
CP600-14..........**$29.99**

The Town and Country 1000

Our biggest backpack!
Available in black or brown.
TC10-560.....~~**$49.99**~~
                $39.99

All of our products are 100% satisfaction guaranteed! Shipping and Handling: Please add 10% to your total.

STUDENT AUDIO **B** Listen and read. What color backpack does the customer want?

Customer Service:	Carry-Time Luggage. Tara speaking. How may I help you?
Customer:	I'd like to place an order for a backpack, please.
Customer Service:	All right. Do you have the item number?
Customer:	Yes, I do. It's TC10-560.
Customer Service:	OK, one TC10-560. That's the Town and Country 1000 backpack.
Customer:	Yes, that's right. I'd like it in black.
Customer Service:	I'm sorry, but the black ones are sold out.*
Customer:	They're sold out?
Customer Service:	Yes, I'm afraid so. Would you be interested in brown?
Customer:	Not really, but thanks anyway.

> **In other words...**
>
> **Apologizing**
> I'm sorry, (but)…
> Yes, I'm afraid so.
> No, I'm afraid not.
> Unfortunately…

*****Idiom note:** sold out = not available anymore; all gone

C Role-play a catalog-order with a partner. Use the example in 1B to make a new conversation.

Partner A: You're the customer. Call the Perfect Pack Company to place an order for a new suitcase. The item number is PL27-120, and you want it in red.

Partner B: You're a customer service representative at Perfect Pack. Item PL27-120 is the Perfect Suitcase 500. Apologize and explain that the red ones are sold out because they are extremely popular. Ask if the customer would be interested in black.

2 Learn *so...that*, *such...that*, and *such a/an...that*

A Study the chart. Complete the sentences below with *so*, *such*, or *such a/an*.

So...that, such...that, such a/an...that	
The prices were **so** high They had **such** high prices	**that** she didn't buy anything.
It was **such an** expensive store	

SALE $588

Notes
• Use *so*, *such*, *such a/an* + *that* to show a result. • Use *so* with an adverb or an adjective. • Use *such* or *such a/an* with an adjective + a singular count noun.

1. That backpack was ____such a____ popular item that they don't have any more.
2. The shirt was _____ small that my son couldn't wear it.
3. This is _____ busy store that it's crowded even at 9:00 in the morning.
4. That CD is _____ quiet that I can't hear it.

B Work with a partner. Write sentences about Alfabuy Department Store. use *so*, *such*, or *such a/an*.

1. Alfabuy is cheap. _Alfabuy is so cheap that you can buy a suit for $50._
2. Alfabuy is a large store. _____
3. Alfabuy has helpful employees. _____
4. Alfabuy has a big parking lot. _____

3 Practice your pronunciation

STUDENT AUDIO **A** Listen to the sentences. Notice how the speakers link the words.

Linked consonants and vowels
When one word ends in a consonant sound and the next word begins with a vowel, the two words are often connected, or linked, in speaking.
I'm afraid not.	He's interested.	Thanks anyway.

STUDENT AUDIO **B** Listen. Draw a line between the linked consonants and vowels.

1. I'd like to place an order.
2. I'm sorry, but we're sold out.
3. It's a really good store.
4. It has our favorite food.

C Read the sentences in 3A and 3B with a partner.

4 Focus on listening

A Look at the picture. Talk about the questions with your class.

1. How does the man feel?
2. What do you think he wants?

B Listen to the conversation. Answer the questions.

1. Who are the two people talking?
2. What does Bill want?

C Listen again. Circle the correct words.

1. Bill ordered the watch after he saw it in (a store / (an advertisement)).
2. He's unhappy because the watch is (dented / scratched).
3. Bill got his order (about a week ago / about three weeks ago).
4. Bill wants to (return / exchange) the watch.
5. Bill needs to write (the item number / the RA number) on the return slip.
6. The number Meg gives Bill is (14-603-4 / 40-703-4).

5 Real-life math

Read the story and answer the question. Explain your answer to your classmates.

Sylvia wants to order two toys for her grandchildren from a catalog. One toy costs $11.95, and the other toy costs $16.95, including tax. The company charges 10% shipping and handling on orders under $50. On orders over $50, shipping and handling is free. Sylvia wants to pay for her order by check.

What amount should Sylvia write the check for? _____

TEST YOURSELF ✔

Role-play a conversation about placing a phone order. Partner A: You're calling a company to order clothing from their catalog. Partner B: You are a customer service representative for the catalog company. You don't have the item in the color the customer wants. Then change roles.

1 Get ready to read

A What does *consumer protection* mean to you?

B Read the definitions. What do you think a *return policy* is?

issue: (verb) to send out
policy: (noun) a rule
rating: (noun) a measurement of how good something is

C Look at the cartoon in the article in 2A. What do you think *Buyer beware* means?

2 Read and respond

A Read the article. Which government offices protect consumers?

Internet Search

Address http://www.consumers.article   ▼ Go

Who's Watching Out for Consumers?

Have you ever heard the saying "Buyer beware!"? It's a warning to consumers to be careful when they buy. That's easy when you're buying a pound of apples or a shirt. However, many products today are so complicated that it's difficult to know what you're looking for. Luckily, consumers have some help.

The U.S. government has several consumer-protection offices. The Consumer Product Safety Commission protects the public from dangerous consumer products. When a product is unsafe, the CPSC may issue a recall. A recall means that consumers can return the product and get their money back.

The Federal Trade Commission also protects consumers. The FTC monitors[1] advertising to be sure that it is truthful. The FTC also regulates[2] product warranties and the information you see on product labels.

Some industries have their own consumer-protection policies. The video game and movie industries, for example, put ratings on their products so that interested parents can decide which movies or games are OK for their children.

Private organizations protect consumers, too. Organizations like Consumers Union compare products and then report the results to their members. These reports help consumers decide which shampoo, insurance plan, or car to buy.

Buyers still need to beware, of course. But it's good to know that you can get help **before** you buy a product and protection **after** you buy it.

[1]monitor: to check or watch something
[2]regulate: to control or supervise through rules or laws

C Work with a partner. Ask and answer the questions.

1. What does the CPSC do?
2. What is a *product recall*?
3. What does the FTC do?
4. How does the video game industry try to help parents?
5. Where can you find ratings on products like cars and insurance policies?

D Study the chart. Complete the sentences below with the correct words.

Word Study: The suffix *-ful*

Add *-ful* to the end of some nouns to form adjectives.
Sometimes there is a spelling change: beau**ty**—beau**tiful**

Noun	Adjective		Noun	Adjective
beauty	beautiful		pain	painful
care	careful		truth	truthful
help	helpful		use	useful

---

1. This tool isn't very __useful__. I'm disappointed in it.
2. Do you think this ad is _____? It seems pretty hard to believe.
3. I burned my hand on my new stove. The burn was very _____.
4. The owner's manual is very well written and clear. It was very _____.
5. Be _____ when you're buying clothes on clearance. Make sure they're not torn or stained.
6. Look at her new earrings! Aren't they _____?

3 Talk it over

Think about the questions. Talk about your ideas with the class.

Do you think the government should protect consumers, or should consumers be responsible for themselves? Why?

BRING IT TO LIFE

Visit several stores or shopping websites. Make notes about their return and exchange policies. Bring your notes to class and compare them with a group. How are they alike? How are they different? Which store or site has the most consumer-friendly policies?

1 Grammar

A Circle the correct adjectives.

1. This video is really (bored /(boring)). I'm taking it back to the library.
2. I was (surprised / surprising) because I usually like movies about adventure.
3. The story in this video was very (disappointed / disappointing).
4. After about 30 minutes, we were completely (confused / confusing).
5. It might be (interested / interesting) if you didn't have anything else to do.

B Order the sentences from the mildest to the strongest. Write 1 for the mildest sentence and 4 for the strongest.

_____ 1. Returning a purchase to this store is really inconvenient.

_1_ 2. Returning a purchase to this store is a little inconvenient.

_____ 3. Returning a purchase to this store is extremely inconvenient.

_____ 4. Returning a purchase to this store is pretty inconvenient.

C Complete the sentences with *so, such,* or *such a/an*.

1. Savers City is a good store. They have __such__ great prices that I always save money.
2. They have _____ excellent guarantee that I never have a problem with returns.
3. I got this shirt there yesterday. It was _____ cheap that I had to buy it!
4. This sofa had _____ big stain on it that they were selling it "as is" for 75% off.
5. It was _____ nice color that we decided to buy it.

D Match the parts of the sentences.

_e_ 1. This website is so helpful that   a. I'm not confused anymore.

_____ 2. It has interesting information about   b. when I save a lot of money!

_____ 3. It was a little confusing at first, but   c. I told my friends about it.

_____ 4. It's extremely   d. easy to use.

_____ 5. It has such good advice that   e. I use it all the time.

_____ 6. I get really excited   f. products and companies.

2 Group work

A Work with 2–3 classmates. Write a 6–8 line conversation between the people in the picture. Share your conversation with the class.

A: *How can I help you today?*
B: *I'm having a problem with one of your products.*
A: *All right. What seems to be the problem?*
B: *Well,…*

B Interview 3 classmates. Write their answers.

1. What was your best shopping experience? What was your worst?
2. What shopping advice would you give someone who has just moved to your area? Why?
3. Would you prefer to buy shoes at a thrift store or from a catalog? Why?

C Talk about the answers with your class.

PROBLEM SOLVING

 A Listen and read about Tonya.

Last week, Tonya's neighbors had a yard sale. Tonya doesn't know her neighbors very well, but she went to the yard sale and bought a vacuum cleaner for $25. When she got it home, however, she noticed some problems with it. It made a lot of noise, and it didn't really clean very well. Tonya knows that there are no guarantees at yard sales, but she is unhappy that her neighbors didn't tell her about the problems.

B Work with your classmates. Answer the questions.

1. What is Tonya's problem?
2. What should she do? Think of 3 possible solutions for Tonya.
3. Write a short letter to Tonya. Tell her what you think she should do.

Take Care!

FOCUS ON
- medical histories
- making healthy changes
- forms of advice
- a doctor's visit
- health insurance

LESSON 1 Vocabulary

1 Learn health vocabulary

A Talk about the questions with your class.

1. What are some things people do to stay healthy and live a long life?
2. Who is the oldest person you have ever known? How old is he or she?

B Work with your classmates. Match the words with the pictures.

Althea Jones' Long Life

____ active lifestyle	____ good nutrition	____ prenatal care
____ dental checkups	_1_ heredity	____ yearly physicals
____ early detection	____ medical screenings	

C Listen and check. Then read the new words with a partner.

D Work with a partner. Write other health history words you know. Check your words in a dictionary.

☑ Identify and use health vocabulary to talk about personal health

E Work with a partner. Talk about the questions. Use the words in 1B.

1. What has helped Althea Jones live a long life?
2. What did Althea Jones do when she was pregnant?
3. How does Ms. Jones try to prevent health problems?

2 Learn vocabulary for medical conditions

A Study the medical history form. Circle 5 problems Althea Jones has had.

MEDICAL HISTORY FORM						
Name: Althea Jones			**Physician:** Dr. Suveena Herat			
	Yes	**No**			**Yes**	**No**
Childhood diseases			Persistent cold (more than 2 weeks)		☐	☑
measles	☑	☐	**Chronic** cough (cough that does not get better)		☐	☑
mumps	☐	☑	High blood pressure		☐	☑
chicken pox	☑	☐	Heart problems or heart **disease**		☐	☑
Recent weight gain or loss	☐	☑	**Weakness** in arms or legs		☑	☐
Frequent or **severe** headaches	☐	☑	Chest pain or other **symptoms** of heart disease		☐	☑
Allergies to medications	☑	☐	Family history of heart disease (Explain below.)		☑	☐
If yes, which medications?			My mother and grandmother had heart disease.			
I'm **allergic** to penicillin.						

B Work with a partner. Complete the doctor's notes with the words in 2A.

> Ms. Jones is very healthy. She maintains an active lifestyle and has had regular medical screenings. There is a family history of heart _____disease_____.
> (1)
> However, Ms. Jones has no _____ of heart disease. She has
> (2)
> some _____ in one leg. She sometimes has headaches, but they
> (3)
> are mild, not _____. She sometimes coughs, but she doesn't
> (4)
> have a _____ cough. It goes away with medication. She is
> (5)
> _____ to penicillin.
> (6)

C Talk about the questions with your class.

1. Which is more important to a person's health—heredity or lifestyle? Why?
2. What are the advantages of checkups and medical screenings?

TEST YOURSELF ✔

Partner A: Read the vocabulary words in 1B to a partner. Partner B: Close your book. Write the words. Ask your partner for help with spelling as necessary. Then change roles. Partner B: Use the words in 2A.

1 Read a personal letter about healthy changes

A Talk about the questions with your class.

1. What are some examples of changes that people make to improve their health?
2. Would you be comfortable giving health advice to a friend? To a classmate? To a family member? Why or why not?

B Listen and read the letter.

Dear Marisol,

Thank you very much for your letter. It was great to hear all your news. Wow—things have been really busy at your house!

I've been busy, too. A few months ago, I realized I was feeling tired all the time. So I decided to cut back on* sugar. I used to have a real sweet tooth, and I ate a lot of candy and sweet snacks. My plan was to cut out* sugar on weekdays.

At first, it wasn't easy. I thought, "Oh, just one candy bar won't hurt," but after a few weeks, that changed. I didn't want sweet snacks all the time. Once or twice on the weekends was enough. Since I made that change, I've felt so much better! I have more energy, and I sleep better, too. It's great!

Well, it's time for me to go to class. Please say hello to your family for me, and write again soon!

Take care,
Christina

> **Writer's note**
>
> Letters often start with a comment about the letter the writer is answering.

*Idiom notes: cut back on = use less of
cut out = stop using completely

C Check your understanding. Circle the correct words.

1. Christina last heard from Marisol by ((letter) / phone).
2. (Marisol / Christina) was feeling tired a lot.
3. Christina decided to (cut back on / cut out) sugar during the week.
4. Christina still eats (some / a lot of) sweet snacks on the weekends.
5. Eating less sugar has made Christina (have more energy / need less sleep).

2 Write a personal letter

 A **Talk about the questions with your class.**

1. What lifestyle changes are easy to make? What changes are difficult? Why?
2. Name two ways to break a bad habit or to start a good habit.

B **You received a letter from a friend. Write a personal letter back to your friend about a lifestyle change you have made. Use the model in 1B and the questions and suggestions below to help you.**

Paragraph 1: Respond to the news you got from your friend in his or her last letter.

Paragraph 2: Tell your friend about a problem you have had. What did you do about it? What change did you make in your life?

Paragraph 3: How did you feel about making this change at first? How do you feel about it now? Did making the change help you?

Closing: End your letter in a friendly way.

> Dear (friend's name),
>   Thank you very much for your letter. It was great to hear from you...

C **Use the checklist to edit your writing. Check (✔) the true sentences.**

Editing checklist	
1. I started with a comment about the letter I received.	
2. I wrote about a problem I had.	
3. I wrote about how making a change helped me.	
4. I indented each paragraph.	

D **Exchange letters with a partner. Read and comment on your partner's letter.**

1. Point out one idea you think is interesting.
2. Ask your partner a question about the change he or she wrote about.

TEST YOURSELF ✔

Write a new letter. Tell a friend about another change you made to improve your health, change your lifestyle, or reduce stress.

1 Learn different forms of advice

A Look at the pictures. What advice does the doctor give each patient?

B Study the chart. Circle the 2 sentences in 1A that give the strongest advice.

Advice with *should, had better,* and *ought to*					
You	**should** **ought to**	eat more healthy food. exercise more.	You	**shouldn't**	stay up so late.
You	**had better**	drink less coffee.	You	**had better not**	go to school today.

Notes
• Use *should* and *ought to* to give advice. They mean the same thing. • In the U.S., people don't usually use *ought to* in negative statements. • Use *had better* to give strong advice or to tell someone to do something.

C Complete the statements with *had better* or *had better not*.

1. You ___had better___ see a doctor. You don't look well.

2. You _____ go to work today. You should stay home when you have a fever.

3. You _____ call in sick. Your boss needs to know that you're not coming in.

4. You need to rest. You _____ go out until you feel better.

5. You _____ take your medicine. The doctor said that it will help you get better.

D Match the sentences.

_c_ 1. You look very tired today.   a. She shouldn't eat so many candy bars.

____ 2. She eats a lot of sugar.   b. We ought to exercise every day.

____ 3. Our diet isn't very healthy.   c. You should get more sleep.

____ 4. We need to lose weight.   d. She'd better see a doctor.

____ 5. She always has headaches.   e. We should eat more fresh vegetables.

E Get the form. Work with your class. Correct the sentences.

1. You should to walk every day.   _____

2. You ought talk to a doctor.   _____

3. You better drink a lot of water. _____

2 Learn the difference between forms of advice

A Study the chart. Write 2 more examples of the strongest types of advice.

Advice and strong advice		
mild ↑ strong stronger ↓	should, ought to had better must, have to, have got to	You **should** eat more vegetables. You**'d better** take a vacation. You **have to** take this medicine.

Note
Have got to is as strong as *have to* and *must,* but is less formal.

B Categorize the advice. Write *M* for mild, *S* for strong, or *SR* for stronger.

_SR_ 1. You've got to see a doctor.   ____ 3. You must see a doctor.

____ 2. You'd better see a doctor.   ____ 4. You should see a doctor.

C Write your own advice. Use the advice words from the chart in 2A in each sentence.

should	~~ought to~~	had better	have to

1. A classmate says, "I'm sick. I have a fever."

   You say, "_You ought to go home_____."

2. A co-worker says, "I just cut my hand. It's bleeding."

   You say, "_____."

3. Your teacher says, "I have a cold."

   You say, "_____."

4. Your friend says, "I hurt my finger. I can't move it."

   You say, "_____."

3 Grammar listening

 Listen to two speakers give advice. Who gives stronger advice? Check (✔)
Speaker A **or** *Speaker B*.

	Speaker A	Speaker B
1.	✔	
2.		
3.		
4.		
5.		
6.		

4 Practice *should, had better, have to,* and *must*

A **Think about your answers to these questions.**

1. In your opinion, what are some things people should do when they have colds?
2. What is one thing people ought to do for their health? What is one thing they should not do?
3. Imagine that a friend wants to lose weight. Talk about what he or she had better do.

B **Work with a partner. Ask and answer the questions.**

A: *What do you think people should do when they have colds?*
B: *I think they should rest.*

C **Talk about your ideas with the class.**

We think that people should rest and wash their hands when they have colds.

TEST YOURSELF ✔

Close your book. Write 5 or more sentences on how people can improve their health. Use different forms of advice.

1 Learn to ask and answer questions at a doctor's office

A Look at the pictures. Listen to the conversations. Then answer the questions below with your classmates.

1. What health goal does each person have?
2. What does the doctor recommend?

B Listen and read. How do you know the patient is listening carefully?

Doctor: You've lost some weight since your last checkup, Al.

Patient: Well, I'm trying to exercise more. I'm concerned about diabetes*.

Doctor: Does diabetes run in your family?

Patient: Yes. My father has it. I want to do what I can to prevent it.

Doctor: Well, keeping your weight down is an excellent first step. Cutting back on sugar can help, too.

Patient: OK. Is there anything else you'd recommend?

Doctor: Healthy eating is important. Try to get four or five servings of vegetables a day.

Patient: So I should continue exercising, cut back on sugar, and eat more vegetables.

Doctor: Yes, that's it. And it's great that you're thinking about prevention now.

> **In other words...**
>
> **Confirming advice**
> So I should...
> So I need to...
> So I'm supposed to...
> So I have to...

*diabetes = a disease that causes a person's body to have trouble controlling the amount of sugar in the blood

C Role-play a checkup with a partner. Use the example in 1B to make a new conversation.

Partner A: You're the doctor. Comment on your patient's high blood pressure. Listen to your patient and ask if high blood pressure runs in the family. Explain that cutting out salt is a good first step. Suggest cutting back on tea and coffee too. Recommend swimming or cycling.

Partner B: You're the patient. Tell your doctor that you're eating less salt because you're concerned about high blood pressure. Your mother has it. Ask the doctor for other recommendations to help you. Confirm your doctor's advice.

✔ Ask and answer questions about health issues **123**

2 Learn verbs with gerunds and infinitives

A Study the chart. Give 5 examples of an infinitive. Give 5 examples of a gerund.

Verbs with gerunds and infinitives			
Verb + gerund	quit consider	avoid feel like	He **quit smoking** ten years ago. I'd **consider joining** a gym.
Verb + infinitive	decide plan	agree need	We **decided to limit** sugar in our coffee. She's **planning to make** some changes.
Verb + gerund OR infinitive	start like	continue prefer	I've **started walking** to work every day. I've **started to walk** to work every day.

B Work with a partner. Complete the sentences with the infinitive or gerund form of the verbs in parentheses. Some items have two correct answers.

1. Why did he quit _____exercising_____? (exercise)
2. Which types of exercise do you like _____? (do)
3. What did you decide _____ in your diet? (change)
4. I'm going to start _____ more healthy food. (eat)

C Work with a group. Look at the picture. Give George some advice. Use the verbs in 1A.

George should quit / start...
He shouldn't continue...
He needs...

3 Practice your pronunciation

A Listen to the pronunciation of *s* and *ch* in these words. How are they different?

Pronunciation of *s*		Pronunciation of *ch*	
since	sugar	checkup	headache

B Circle the sound of the underlined letters in these words. Then listen and check.

1. in<u>s</u>urance (s /(sh))   3. stoma<u>ch</u>   (ch / k)   5. <u>ch</u>ange   (ch / k)
2. <u>s</u>erving (s / sh)   4. ea<u>ch</u>   (ch / k)   6. <u>ch</u>ronic   (ch / k)

C Say the sentences with a partner. Then listen and check your pronunciation.

1. She should not serve sugar.   3. I have to change my health insurance.
2. She has a stomachache.   4. I shouldn't eat it. I'm sure it's sweet.

4 Focus on listening

A Look at the poster. Talk about the questions with your class.

1. Have you ever had a tetanus shot? Why?
2. How do you feel about getting shots?

B Listen to the conversation. Work with a partner. Ask and answer the questions.

1. Why is Mr. Gomez visiting the doctor?
2. How does Mr. Gomez feel about getting a shot?

C Listen again. Circle the correct words.

1. Mr. Gomez cut himself when he was working in the (house / garden).
2. The doctor gives Mr. Gomez antibiotic (ointment / pills) for the cut.
3. Mr. Gomez had a tetanus shot (less than 10 / more than 20) years ago.
4. The doctor gives Mr. Gomez (two shots / one shot) on this visit.
5. Mr. Gomez (has to / doesn't have to) see the doctor again next week.

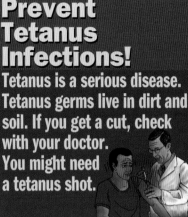

Prevent Tetanus Infections!
Tetanus is a serious disease. Tetanus germs live in dirt and soil. If you get a cut, check with your doctor. You might need a tetanus shot.

5 Real-life math

Read Mr. Gomez's immunization record and answer the questions. Explain your answers to your classmates.

PERSONAL IMMUNIZATION RECORD					
Name: Ernesto Gomez	DOB: 6/19/50				
Immunization		Received on:			
Td[1] (Tetanus and Diptheria)		9/79	9/89		
Flu[2]					

[1]Every 10 years for life
[2]After age 50

1. Mr. Gomez is getting a Td immunization today. When will he need one again?
2. Why does Mr. Gomez need a flu shot?

TEST YOURSELF ✔

Role-play a conversation. Partner A: Ask your friend for advice about staying healthy. Then confirm the advice. Partner B: You have a healthy lifestyle. Ask your friend questions and give advice about good health habits. Then change roles.

1 Get ready to read

 Why is health insurance important?

 Read the definitions. Name 3 kinds of medical specialists.

cover: (verb) to pay for

referral: (noun) a suggestion or permission to visit a doctor or get a screening

specialist: (noun) a doctor who is an expert in one kind of medicine or health care

 Look at the title and the headings in the article in 2A. Answer the questions.

1. What are *FAQs*?
2. What will this article help the reader do?

2 Read and respond

A **Read the article. What are two kinds of health insurance plans?**

FAQs (Frequently Asked Questions) about Health Insurance

Are you trying to choose a health-care plan? These FAQs may help.

1) What kinds of health insurance are available?

There are several options. For example, in a fee-for-service plan, you can see any doctor in any part of the country. The insurance company pays part of the cost (often 80%) and you pay the rest. You pay a monthly premium for the insurance. There's also a deductible, usually about $250.

In a managed-care plan, you see a doctor from the plan's network[1] of doctors. These plans also have a monthly premium. In some plans, you don't have to pay for doctors' visits; in others, you pay a co-payment of $5 or $10 for each doctor's visit.

2) I'm confused by deductibles and co-payments. What's the difference?

Deductibles and co-payments are both amounts of money that you have to pay. A deductible is the amount you pay in a fee-for-service plan before the plan starts to pay (e.g., the first $250 of a bill). A co-payment is the amount you pay for each doctor's visit in a managed-care plan.

3) What should I think about when I choose a plan?

This is an important decision. Before you choose, compare:

Services • What medical care is covered? What isn't? Are chronic conditions and specialists covered? Does the plan have offices near your home or job?

[1]network: a group of people, things, or organizations that work together

Choices • Does the plan include the doctors you want to see? Do you need a referral to see a specialist?

Costs • What would the total cost (the plan, fees, deductibles, etc.) be for you and your family?

Choosing health care, like choosing a good doctor, isn't easy. The more you know, the better your choice will be.

Adapted from: *http://www.ahrq.gov*

B Listen and read the article again.

C Write the number of the FAQ that answers these questions. Then ask and answer the questions with a partner.

___1___ 1. How are fee-for-service plans and managed-care plans different?

_____ 2. What is a deductible?

_____ 3. What should I look at when I am trying to choose a health plan?

_____ 4. How much does it cost to see the doctor in a managed-care plan?

D Study the chart. Complete the sentences below.

Word Study: Verbs for talking about health and illness				
feel well/better	get sick	have { a physical / an illness	see { a doctor / a dentist	take { medicine / vitamins

1. When are you going to ___see___ the ear, nose, and throat specialist?

2. I wash my hands often because I don't want to _____ sick.

3. Do you _____ a cold? I hope you _____ better soon.

4. When you _____ your doctor, he'll probably tell you to _____ vitamins.

3 Talk it over

Think about the questions. Talk about your ideas with the class.

1. Who should pay for health insurance—employers, the government, or people? Why?

2. What do you think the saying "An ounce of prevention is worth a pound of cure" means? Do you agree with the saying? Why or why not? Give examples.

BRING IT TO LIFE

Find an article on the Internet or in the library about preventing colds.
Bring your article to class and share the information in small groups.

1 Grammar

A Circle the correct words.

1. Luz hurt her back. She (**had better** / had better not) see her doctor.

2. She (has got to / had better not) lift anything heavy.

3. Her doctor said she (has to / had better not) be careful when she exercises.

4. Her doctor also said that she (ought to / had better not) go back to work until she feels better.

5. She (ought to / had better not) call her boss.

B Read the information. Which sentences are closest in meaning? Circle *a* or *b*.

1. You really need to brush your teeth often.

   a. You must brush your teeth often.

   b. You must not brush your teeth often.

2. It's a good idea to brush at least twice a day.

   a. You shouldn't brush twice a day.

   b. You ought to brush twice a day.

3. Too much sugar is bad for your teeth.

   a. You shouldn't eat foods with a lot of sugar.

   b. You ought to eat foods with a lot of sugar.

4. It's important to see the dentist every six months.

   a. You've got to see the dentist every six months.

   b. You shouldn't see the dentist every six months.

C Complete the sentences with the gerund or infinitive form of the verb in parentheses. Some items have two correct answers.

1. Jean and Lars decided ____to make____ some changes in their lives. (make)

2. They considered _____ a health club, but it was a little expensive. (join)

3. So they started _____ their bikes for exercise. (ride)

4. They agreed _____ a salad with dinner every night. (have)

5. Jean says she is going to quit _____ so much meat. (eat)

6. Lars says he is going to start _____ more water and less soda. (drink)

2 Group work

A Work with 2–3 classmates. Write a 6–8 line conversation between the people in the picture. Share your conversation with the class.

A: *You're in very good health. Do you have any health concerns?*
B: *Well, I'm worried about...*

B Interview 3 classmates. Write their answers.

1. How much should people have to pay for health care? Why?
2. Should people with healthy lifestyles pay less for health care? Why or why not?
3. If you could give everyone advice on how to prevent health problems, what would your advice be?

C Talk about the answers with your class.

PROBLEM SOLVING

A Listen and read about Ivan.

Ivan is worried about his sister, Katya. He thinks that Katya doesn't pay enough attention to her health. Ivan believes in preventing health problems, and he exercises and eats a healthy diet. Katya doesn't exercise. She eats fast-food for dinner several times a week, and she doesn't have health insurance at her job. Katya is an independent person who doesn't like it when people try to tell her what to do. Ivan wants Katya to be healthy, but he doesn't know how to help.

B Work with your classmates. Answer the questions.

1. What is Ivan's problem?
2. What do you think he should do? Think of 2 or 3 solutions to the problem.
3. Make two lists—a list of things Ivan could say to Katya, and a list of things he should *not* say.

UNIT **10**

FOCUS ON
- community involvement and community services
- community issues
- indirect questions
- addressing community problems
- environmental issues

Get Involved!

LESSON **1**   Vocabulary

1 Learn community-involvement vocabulary

A Talk about the questions with your class.

1. What do you like about your community? What don't you like?
2. What makes a community a good place to live?

B Work with your classmates. Match the words with the pictures.

| ____ develop a plan | ____ get approval | ____ implement the plan |
| ____ discuss the issue | _1_ identify a problem | ____ propose a solution |

C Listen and check. Then read the new words with a partner.

D Work with a partner. Write other community-involvement words you know. Check your words in a dictionary.

E Work with a partner. Ask and answer the questions.

1. What steps should you follow to identify and solve problems in a community?
2. Who should be involved in each step? Neighbors? Community leaders?

2 Learn community-services vocabulary

A Study the community services directory. Which office do you think gets the most telephone calls? Why?

Department / Telephone Extension	Services	Department / Telephone Extension	Services
Administration x5510	mayor, council, city manager	Parks & Recreation x5514	sports, art, music programs, community centers
Child Care Services x5511	low-cost daycare	Public Safety x5515	crime prevention, fire safety
Health Services x5512	low-cost health clinics	Public Works x5516	street and lighting maintenance, building permits
Legal Services x5513	low-cost law clinics	Senior Services x5517	senior centers, lunch programs

B Work with a partner. Complete the sentences with names of the departments. Use the words in 2A.

1. Isabel wants to talk to the city manager. She'll call _Administration_.
2. A traffic light is broken on Main Street. I'll call _____.
3. Yosef wants information about community centers. He'll call _____.
4. Maria wants information on low-cost daycare. She'll call _____.
5. Gary wants to know how to reduce crime. He'll call _____.
6. We want to know where the nearest low-cost health clinic is. We'll call _____.
7. Paco needs some low-cost legal help. He'll call _____.
8. I want information on lunch programs for my grandmother. I'll call _____.

C Talk about the questions with your class.

Which community services are the most important to you?
Which are the least important to you? Why?

TEST YOURSELF ✔

Close your book. Categorize the new words in two lists: *Community Involvement* and *Community Services*. Check your spelling in a dictionary. Compare your lists with a partner.

1 Read about a community issue

A   Talk about the questions with your class.

1. How do people help improve their communities?
2. Have you ever tried to solve a problem in your community, school, or workplace? If so, what was the problem? What did you do?

B   Listen and read the letter.

Alan Hart
1856 Arroyo St.
Edison, TX 75002

July 12, 2007

Ms. Toya Butler
County Council Member, District 3
3300 Hilltop Road
Edison, TX 75002

Dear Ms. Butler:

I am writing to ask for your help with a problem in our community. I live in the Melrose neighborhood, near the intersection of Pine and Arroyo streets.

I am very concerned about people who walk across the street at this intersection. The traffic light changes too quickly. I think we need to increase the time that the light stays red. Older people who walk with canes or walkers cannot make it across the street in time. Parents with children also have a difficult time. I have timed the light and it changes from green to yellow to red in 13 seconds. If the light stayed red for 5 more seconds, everyone would be able to cross safely.

I would like to invite you to visit our neighborhood to see the problem for yourself. Please contact me at (972) 555-1409. I look forward to hearing from you.

Sincerely,
Alan Hart
Alan Hart

> **Writer's note**
>
> Each paragraph of this letter has a special purpose:
> 1. Introduction
> 2. Explanation
> 3. Invitation

C   Check your understanding. Work with a partner. Ask and answer the questions.

1. How does Alan Hart start his letter? Why?
2. What two examples show that the problem is serious?
3. What are two things he wants?

2 Write a letter about a problem in the community

 A **Talk about the questions with your class.**

1. What are some things you would like to improve in your community? Why?
2. Who could you write to about these situations?

B **Write a letter about one of the problems you described in 2A.**
Use the model in 1B and the questions below to help you.

To start: Write your return address, the date, and the mailing address
               at the top of your letter.
               Write *Dear* and the title and last name of the addressee.

Paragraph 1: Why are you writing? Where is the problem?

Paragraph 2: What is the problem? What are some examples
               that show that the problem is serious?

Paragraph 3: What do you want the person to do?
               How can the person contact you?

To close: Write a closing. Sign and print your name.

	(Your address)
	(Receiver's name and address)
	Dear _____ :
	I am writing to…

C **Use the checklist to edit your writing. Check (✔) the true sentences.**

Editing checklist	
1. My letter includes the name and address of the person I am writing to.	
2. I introduced the problem in the first paragraph.	
3. I explained the problem and gave examples in the second paragraph.	
4. I included my contact information in the third paragraph.	

D **Exchange letters with a partner. Read and comment on your partner's letter.**

1. Point out a good example in your partner's letter of how serious the problem is.
2. Ask a question about the problem your partner described.

TEST YOURSELF ✔

Write a new letter about a problem in the area near your school or workplace.

---

1 Learn indirect information questions

A Look at the letter to the editor and the editorial cartoon. What do the letter writer and the cartoonist disagree about?

LETTER TO THE EDITOR

Do you know what our city's biggest problem is? We need money for schools, not for public transportation!

B Study the charts. Underline the 2 indirect questions in 1A.

INDIRECT INFORMATION QUESTIONS

Direct information question	Indirect information question
When **is** the bus **coming**?	Do you know when the bus **is coming**?
Where **do** the buses **stop**?	Could you please tell me where the buses **stop**?
What **does** the mayor **want**?	Do you have any idea what the mayor **wants**?
What **were** the issues?	Do you know what the issues **were**?
How **did** this **happen**?	Can you tell me how this **happened**?

Note
Indirect questions sound more polite than *Yes/No* or information questions.

C Match each situation with an indirect question.

You don't know...

_b_ 1. the location of the bus stop.   a. Do you have any idea why the bus is late?

____ 2. the reason the bus isn't here yet.   b. Could you tell me where the bus stop is?

____ 3. the bus schedule.   c. Do you know which buses stop here?

____ 4. which buses use this bus stop.   d. Can you tell me when the bus will come?

D Get the form. Work with your class. Correct the indirect questions.

1. Do you know where is the park? _Do you know where the park is?_

2. Do you know what does want the teacher? _____

3. Could you tell me where is the post office? _____

4. Can you tell me how do you get to city hall? _____

☑ Use and respond to indirect questions to talk about community issues

E **Read the answers. Then complete the indirect question. Practice reading the questions and answers with a partner.**

1. Do you know _____ when the meeting is _____? (when)

   I think the meeting is at 6 p.m.

2. Do you know _____? (where)

   It's in Room A.

3. Do you have any idea _____? (what)

   I believe the mayor wants to talk about the budget.

4. Could you please tell me _____? (what)

   The mayor's proposal cuts bus service.

5. Can you tell me _____? (which)

   The city cut the parks, transportation, and senior services budgets.

2 Learn indirect *Yes/No* questions

A **Study the charts. What word means the same as *if*?**

Direct *Yes/No* questions	Indirect *Yes/No* questions		
Is the bus **coming**?	Can you tell me Could you tell me Do you know	**if** **whether**	the bus **is coming**?
Did they **get** approval?	Can you tell me Could you tell me Do you know	**if** **whether**	they **got** approval?

B **Read the direct questions. Then complete the indirect questions.**

1. Is the meeting at 5:00?

   Do you know _if the meeting is at 5:00_____?

2. Did they discuss the issue?

   Could you tell me _____?

3. Are they going to approve the budget cut?

   Do you know _____?

4. Was the mayor at the meeting?

   Do you have any idea _____?

5. Did the meeting end on time?

   Can you tell me _____?

6. Are they going to meet next month?

   Could you tell me _____?

3 Grammar listening

 Listen to the speakers. What does the person want to know? Circle *a* or *b*.

1. a. When is the next public works committee meeting?
   b. Where is the next public works committee meeting?

2. a. Why is the law clinic closed?
   b. When is the law clinic closed?

3. a. Did you talk about childcare services?
   b. Who do I talk to about childcare services?

4. a. Where is the nearest senior center in your city?
   b. Does your city have any senior centers?

5. a. What does the city manager want?
   b. Where did the city manager go?

6. a. Did the public safety committee discuss my idea?
   b. When did the public safety committee discuss my idea?

4 Practice indirect questions

A **Write at least 5 indirect questions about services in your community.**

Do you know where the senior center is?

B **Work with your classmates. Ask and answer each other's questions. Talk to at least 5 people.**

A: *Do you know where…*
B: *I'm not sure, but…*

C **Take turns writing and correcting the indirect questions on the board.**

TEST YOURSELF ✔

Close your book. Write 6 new indirect questions about services or programs at your school.

1 Learn to talk about a problem in the community

A Look at the notice. Listen to the phone calls. How do the callers feel about the plans for the apartment building and the Jobs for Teens program?

NOTICE OF PUBLIC HEARINGS

Tomas Noyes, City Clerk, City of Dawson   **November 15**

ISSUE: Plan to build an apartment building next to the 40th Street Park.
Date: Nov. 20

ISSUE: Proposal to reduce the Summer Jobs for Teens Program from 500 to 150 participants.
Date: Nov. 28

ISSUE: Proposal to close the Community Police Station in the Hilltop Apartments.
Date: Dec. 12

All hearings will take place at 7 p.m. in the Council Chamber, on the 1st floor of the Municipal Building, 440 State St. Interested residents are encouraged to attend and comment on the proposals.

B Listen and read. How does Maria feel about the Hilltop Police Station?

City Clerk: City clerk's office. Can I help you?

Caller: Hi. This is Maria Delgado. I'm calling because I heard that the city wants to close the Hilltop Police Station. Can you tell me if that's true?

City Clerk: Yes, it is.

Caller: Why would they do that? It's an important service.

City Clerk: I know what you mean. Listen, there's a public hearing on the issue at 7 p.m. on December 12th, in the Council Chamber.

Caller: Really? Hmmm… I'm not sure where that is.

City Clerk: It's in the Municipal Building, on the third floor.

Caller: Thanks. I'll be there. I want to put in my two cents!*

*Idiom note: put in (my) two cents = give (my) opinion

> **In other words…**
>
> **Showing understanding**
>
> I know what you mean.
> I hear what you're saying.
> I understand what you're saying.

C Role-play a phone call to the city clerk's office with a partner. Use the example in 1B to make a new conversation.

Partner A: Call the city clerk because you heard that the city is planning to close the Troy Street Library. You think the library is really important. Say that you don't know where the community meeting is.

Partner B: You're the city clerk. Show your understanding to the caller. Say that there's a community meeting about the issue next Wednesday at the Troy Street Library, on the second floor.

☑ Call a community official about an issue or event   **137**

2 Learn statements with *wh-* and *if/whether* phrases

A Study the chart and the picture. What is the man's problem?

Statements with *wh-* and *if/whether* phrases	
He doesn't know	**where** the community meeting is.
He has no idea	**what** the meeting is about.
He's not sure	**when** the meeting starts.
He can't remember	**if** the meeting starts at 7 p.m.
He forgot	**whether** the meeting starts at 7 p.m.

Note

Use a *wh-* OR an *if/whether* phrase after certain expressions to talk about things you don't know for certain.

B Work with a partner. Complete the sentences. Circle the correct words.

Ed: I want to go to the meeting, but I don't know when (does it start / (it starts)).
(1)

Mai: It's at 7:00, but I have no idea what (is it / it's) about.
(2)

Ed: It's about the health clinic. I'm not sure what (the issues are / are the issues).
(3)

Mai: I'll bet it's about the budget. I can't remember if (they cut / did they cut) it.
(4)

Ed: I don't know what (do you think / you think), but I think we ought to go.
(5)

C Work with a partner. Talk about the people in 2B.

A: *Ed doesn't know when the community meeting starts.*
B: *Mai has…*

3 Practice your pronunciation

 A Listen to these long sentences. Notice where the speakers pause.

1. I'm calling because I heard that ∧ the city wants to close the Hilltop Police Station.
2. There's a public hearing on the issue ∧ at 7 p.m. tonight, ∧ in the Council Chamber.

 B Listen and mark the pauses (∧) in these sentences.

1. Older people who walk with canes or walkers cannot make it across the street in time.
2. The council members discuss the issue to try to find a solution that works for everyone.

C Practice the sentences in 3A and 3B with a partner.

4 Focus on listening

A Talk about the questions with your class.

Budget Hearing Tonight!
Open to the Public

1. Why do people attend community meetings and public hearings?
2. How can people get information about meetings and hearings?

B Listen to the recorded message. Circle the correct meeting day, date, time, and location.

1. a. Tuesday   b. Thursday   3. a. 7:30 p.m.   b. 7:00 p.m.
2. a. March 23   b. May 23   4. a. Room 210   b. Hearing Room

C Listen again. Complete the directions with the words you hear.

1. To get to city hall, take the _____F4_____ bus.
2. Go _____ one block to Beech Street to get to the parking lot.
3. Take the elevator to the _____ floor.
4. Follow the signs to the _____.
5. It will be on your _____, after Room _____.

5 Real-life math

Study the pie chart of East Port's annual budget and answer the questions. Explain your answers to your classmates.

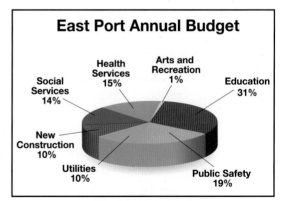

East Port Annual Budget

Social Services 14%
Health Services 15%
Arts and Recreation 1%
Education 31%
New Construction 10%
Utilities 10%
Public Safety 19%

1. Which two programs together use half of the city's budget? _____
2. If the total city budget is one hundred million dollars, how much is the city spending on arts and recreation in a year? _____

TEST YOURSELF ✔

Role-play a phone call about a community issue. Partner A: Call the city clerk. The city is planning to put up a stop sign at a dangerous intersection, but you think it should be a stop light. Partner B: You are the city clerk. Tell the caller about the Traffic Safety Committee meeting next week. Then change roles.

1 Get ready to read

A What are some ways that communities keep parks and open areas clean?

B Read the definitions. Which word can mean *legally take care of*?

adopt: (verb) to be responsible for someone or something that isn't yours
announce: (verb) to say; make a public statement
fine: (noun) money you have to pay for breaking a law

C Look at the title of the newspaper article and the section headings in 2A. Answer the questions.

1. Which part of the newspaper do you think this article is from?
2. What do you think *dumping* means?

2 Read and respond

A Read the article. What three things can Riverview residents do to get involved?

Community Involvement: Something for Everyone!

What makes our city a great place to live? Is it a great location? Good neighbors? Good services? Yes—but it's also the involvement of residents in the life of the community. If you want to get involved, but don't know how you can help, here are three easy ways to get started.

Adopt-a-Road

The Riverview city council has just announced a new Adopt-a-Road program. Under this program, community groups and companies can "adopt" a section of a city or country road. The group picks up litter along the road four times a year, and in return, the group's name is posted along the road. Support the new program by adopting a road and keeping it clean.

Support our Plan to Change Dumping Laws

Our country highways and natural areas become dirty and dangerous when people dump old furniture, building materials, tires, or other trash along the road or in the river. Riverview has a law against illegal dumping, but the fine is only $50. Under the Environmental Committee's proposed new law, the fine would be raised to $500. Let your council member know that you support increased fines for illegal dumping. Make your voice heard!

Participate in Community Clean-Up Days

Four times a year, Riverview sponsors[1] Community Clean-Up Days. Residents help clean up parks, plant trees, and repair community buildings. If you aren't sure when the

---

[1]sponsor: to organize; support

next Community Clean Up is, check the city's website at www.riverside.city. Volunteer, and get children to volunteer. You're never too young, or too old, to play an active part[2] in your community!

A great community is everyone's responsibility. Let's all get involved in making Riverview an even better place to live.

[2]to play an active part: to be involved; to participate

B **Listen and read the newspaper article again.**

C **Check your understanding. Work with a partner. Ask and answer the questions.**

1. In the Adopt-a-Road program, what does a group do? What does the group get?
2. Why is dumping a problem?
3. What solution did the Environmental Committee propose?

D **Fill in the chart with nouns ending in *-ment*. Check your spelling in a dictionary. Then complete the sentences below with nouns from the chart.**

> **Word Study: Changing verbs to nouns with *-ment***
>
> Add *-ment* to the end of some verbs to form nouns: *agree + ment = agreement*
>
> | Verb | Noun | Verb | Noun |
> |------|------|------|------|
> | agree | agreement | govern | _____ |
> | announce | _____ | involve | _____ |
> | assign | _____ | state | _____ |

1. Residents have been calling ____government____ officials about the dumping problem.
2. The council agreed to a budget increase, and the mayor signed the _____.
3. They also made an _____ on TV about a new community clean-up program.
4. It said they wanted to increase residents' _____ in their communities.

3 Talk it over

Think about the questions. Talk about your ideas with the class.

Whose responsibility is it to keep a community clean? Why do you think so?

> **BRING IT TO LIFE**
> How does your area keep roads and parks clean? Use the library or the Internet to find information on clean-up or Adopt-a-Road programs in your area, or on littering and dumping laws in your area. Bring the information to class and tell your classmates about it.

1 Grammar

A **Read the direct questions. Complete the indirect questions.**

1. How do organizations adopt a road?

   Do you know _____ how organizations adopt a road _____?

2. What are the program rules?

   Can you tell me _____?

3. Where is the program office?

   Do you know _____?

4. When did the program begin?

   Do you have any idea _____?

B **Complete the indirect questions with *if* or *what*.**

1. Can you tell me __if__ the senior center is open on weekends?

2. Do you know _____ their hours are?

3. Do you have any idea _____ services they have?

4. Do you know _____ the services are free?

5. Can you tell me _____ all seniors can receive services?

C **Complete the sentences. Use the questions in parentheses.**

1. I'm not sure _____ what the proposal is _____.

   (What is the proposal?)

2. I don't know _____.

   (Which budgets did they cut?)

3. I have no idea _____.

   (Does the committee like the plan?)

4. I don't know _____.

   (Are residents serving on the committee?)

D **Match the parts of the sentences.**

_c_ 1. I have no idea why   a. the budget includes money for fire trucks?

____ 2. I can't remember when   b. a new truck costs.

____ 3. Can you tell me what   c. the mayor wants a new fire truck.

____ 4. I'm not sure how much   d. they purchased the last fire truck.

____ 5. Do you know whether   e. the problem with the old truck is?

2 Group work

A Work with 2–3 classmates. Write a 6–8 line conversation between the people in the picture. Share your conversation with the class.

A: *Excuse me. Do you know where the recycling committee meeting is?*

B: *Yes, it's...*

B Interview 3 classmates. Write their answers.

1. What should people do if they are unhappy about something in their community?
2. What are the most important services a community should have for residents?
3. Which community services should be free? Which ones should residents pay for?

C Talk about the answers with your class.

PROBLEM SOLVING

 A Listen and read about Teresa.

Teresa is worried about problems in her neighborhood. There's always a lot of trash in the streets, the sidewalks are cracked, and there's broken glass in the playground. The trees in the area used to be beautiful, but now they're dying because no one takes care of them. People in the neighborhood have stopped taking walks or spending time together outside, and many people don't know their neighbors.

Teresa believes that her neighborhood can solve its problems. She knows that other communities have neighborhood organizations, and she would like to start one in her area. She has a lot of questions, but she's not sure how to get more information.

B Work with your classmates. Answer the questions.

1. What is Teresa's problem?
2. What could she do? Think of 3 or 4 possible solutions.
3. Write some indirect questions Teresa could ask.

Find It on the Net

FOCUS ON
- Internet and website vocabulary
- changes in technology
- tag questions
- offering and responding to help
- renters' rights

LESSON **1** Vocabulary

1 Learn Internet vocabulary

A Talk about the questions with your class.

1. Do you use a computer? If you do, what do you use it for?
2. What can the Internet help people do?

B Work with your classmates. Match the words with the picture.

_____ cursor	_____ pop-up ad	_____ search box
_____ links	_____ pull-down menu	_1_ URL box
_____ pointer	_____ scroll bar	_____ webpage

C Listen and check. Then read the new words with a partner.

D Work with a partner. Write other Internet words you know. Check your words in a dictionary.

---

144 ✔ Identify and use Internet and website vocabulary

E Work with a partner. Talk about these questions. Use the words in 1B.

1. What parts of a webpage can you click on?
2. Where can you type or enter information on a webpage?
3. What are some things you can do with the cursor and the pointer?

2 Learn website vocabulary

A Look at the website menu. Work with your classmates. Match the links with the definitions.

_b_ 1. information about the organization

_____ 2. the website's first page

_____ 3. a list of questions many people have

_____ 4. the organization's phone number or email address

_____ 5. new information on the website topic

_____ 6. other websites on the same topic

B Work with a partner. Practice the conversation. Use the words in 2A.

A: How do I go to the first page of the website?
B: Click on Home.
A: What happens if I click on What's New?
B: You see new information on the website topic.

C Talk about the questions with your class.

1. What are some websites that people in your class like? Why do they like them?
2. If you had a website, what would you put on it?

TEST YOURSELF ✔

Work with a partner. Partner A: Read the vocabulary words in 1B to your partner. Partner B: Close your book. Write the words. Ask your partner for help with spelling as necessary. Then change roles. Partner B: Use the words in 2A.

1 Read about changes in the use of technology

A **Talk about the questions with your class.**

1. Describe your computer skills. Are you an expert, an experienced user, or a beginner?
2. How has technology changed the way you get information?

STUDENT
AUDIO

B **Listen and read the essay.**

Writer's note

When comparing times, use time expressions to make the times clear for the reader.

Technology Then and Now
By: Pedro Sanchez
Ten years ago, I used technology a lot less in my daily life. I used the Internet at work, but I didn't have it at home. When I needed information from a store or a business, I used to make a phone call. Of course, I could only call during business hours. To shop, I went to a store or ordered by phone, and to get directions, I used a map. It seems funny now to think about how much time it took to get things done.
Today, I use the Internet at home for many of these tasks. I can get information any time. I don't have to wait for business hours. I get a lot of things done without leaving home. I've even taken an online class.
Some things haven't changed, though. I never buy shoes online because I can't try them on, and I still like paper maps better than Internet maps. When it comes to* really important information, I still use the phone. Of course, these days I usually use a cell phone to make those calls!

*Idiom note: when it comes to = when you are talking about

C **Check your understanding. Write T (true), F (false), or NI (no information).**

_F_ 1. Pedro's use of technology hasn't changed much.

_____ 2. Ten years ago, he used a paper map to get directions.

_____ 3. He has had the Internet at home for more than ten years.

_____ 4. He has taken an online English class.

_____ 5. He usually buys shoes on the Internet.

2 Write about using technology

 A **Talk about the questions with your class.**

1. Name some items in your home today that use or connect to a computer.
2. How many of these items did you have ten years ago?

B **Write about changes in your use of technology. Use the model in 1B and the questions below to help you.**

Paragraph 1: What technology did you use ten years ago?
How did you use it?
Paragraph 2: What technology do you use today?
How do you use it?
Paragraph 3: What has not changed?
What do you still do in the same way?

> [Title]
>
> Ten years ago,...
>
>
> Today, I use...
>
>
> Some things...

C **Use the checklist to edit your writing. Check (✔) the true sentences.**

Editing checklist	
1. My first paragraph is about a time in the past.	
2. My second paragraph is about the present.	
3. My third paragraph tells about things that haven't changed.	
4. I used time expressions to make the times clear.	

D **Exchange stories with a partner. Read and comment on your partner's work.**

1. Point out one idea you think is interesting.
2. Ask your partner a question about one of the changes he or she wrote about.

TEST YOURSELF ✔

Write a new paragraph. Compare the technology you use when you study now with the technology you used when you studied ten years ago.

1 Learn tag questions with *be*

A **Read the conversation. Why does Abby go to Leo for help?**

Abby: Hi, Leo. You're an expert with email, aren't you?

Leo: Yes, I am. Why do you ask?

Abby: I'm having trouble emailing the landlord. There's no heat in my apartment.

Leo: That's terrible. The landlord is aware of the problem, isn't he?

Abby: No, he isn't. I want to put it in writing.

Leo: I'd be happy to help you.

B **Study the charts. Underline the 2 tag questions with *be* in the conversation above.**

TAG QUESTIONS AND SHORT ANSWERS WITH *BE*

Affirmative statement	Negative tag	Agreement	Disagreement
You**'re** an expert with email,	**aren't** you?	Yes, I **am**.	No, I**'m not**.
The heat **is** off,	**isn't** it?	Yes, it **is**.	No, it **isn't**.
I **was** helpful,	**wasn't** I?	Yes, you **were**.	No, you **weren't**.

Negative statement	Affirmative tag	Agreement	Disagreement
You**'re not** an expert,	**are** you?	No, I**'m not**.	Yes, I **am**.
The heat **isn't** off,	**is** it?	No, it **isn't**.	Yes, it **is**.
I **wasn't** very helpful,	**was** I?	No, you **weren't**.	Yes, you **were**.

> **Notes**
> - Use a negative tag after an affirmative statement. Negative tags are usually contracted.
>   Ask a negative tag question when you think the answer will be *Yes*.
> - Use an affirmative tag after a negative statement.
>   Ask an affirmative tag question when you think the answer will be *No*.

C **Match the parts of the questions.**

_c_ 1. The heaters are old,   a. were you?

____ 2. This one isn't working very well,   b. isn't she?

____ 3. You're not calling the landlord,   c. aren't they?

____ 4. The landlord was here,   d. are you?

____ 5. She's writing an email,   e. wasn't he?

____ 6. You weren't cold today,   f. is it?

D Complete the sentences with tag questions.

1. The heater is broken, _____ isn't it _____?
2. The repairman wasn't in his shop, _____?
3. It isn't working well, _____?
4. The neighbors were having problems, too, _____?
5. You're going to fix this, _____?
6. We're not being very helpful, _____?

2 Learn tag questions with *do* and *did*

A Study the charts. What punctuation mark comes before a tag?

TAG QUESTIONS AND SHORT ANSWERS WITH *DO* AND *DID*

Affirmative statement	Negative tag	Agreement	Disagreement
You **live** here,	**don't** you?	Yes, I **do**.	No, I **don't**.
He **prefers** email,	**doesn't** he?	Yes, he **does**.	No, he **doesn't**.
The heat **worked** Friday,	**didn't** it?	Yes, it **did**.	No, it **didn't**.

Negative statement	Affirmative tag	Agreement	Disagreement
You **don't live** here,	**do** you?	No, I **don't**.	Yes, I **do**.
He **doesn't like** email,	**does** he?	No, he **doesn't**.	Yes, he **does**.
The heat **didn't work** Friday,	**did** it?	No, it **didn't**.	Yes, it **did**.

B Complete the questions with tags.

1. The landlord fixed this broken window, _____ didn't he _____?
2. You don't want to call him tonight, _____?
3. I needed to talk to him, _____?
4. He doesn't work on Mondays, _____?
5. You didn't send him an email, _____?
6. He usually fixes things right away, _____?

C Get the form. Work with your class. Correct the sentences.

1. You wrote this, did you? _____ You wrote this, didn't you? _____
2. Frank doesn't remember, doesn't he? _____
3. Bonita and Barry got that email, did they? _____
4. Lena uses the Internet, did she? _____
5. Yukio didn't work yesterday, didn't he? _____

3 Grammar listening

🎧 **Listen to the speakers. Choose the correct tags to complete the questions. Circle *a* or *b*.**

1. a. aren't you? *(circled)*
   b. didn't you?

2. a. don't you?
   b. aren't you?

3. a. do you?
   b. did you?

4. a. is it?
   b. does it?

5. a. is she?
   b. isn't she?

6. a. doesn't it?
   b. do they?

7. a. aren't they?
   b. aren't we?

8. a. did we?
   b. didn't we?

9. a. did it?
   b. didn't it?

4 Practice tag questions

A **Choose a partner. Think about your answers to the questions, but don't check your answers yet.**

1. Where is your partner from?
2. What does your partner like to do in his or her free time?
3. How long has your partner studied English?
4. Does your partner live in a house or an apartment?
5. Can your partner use a computer?

B **Work with your partner. Ask tag questions to check your answers in 1A. Answer your partner's questions. Try to add extra information.**

A: *You're from Sri Lanka, aren't you?*
B: *Yes, I am. I came here last year.*
A: *You like to cook, don't you?*
B: *No, actually, I don't. I…*

> **Need help?**
>
> After a short answer, people often add extra information. This helps keep the conversation going.

C **Test your classmates. Ask questions about your partner and answer your classmates' tag questions.**

A: *Where's Adil from?*
B: *He's from Thailand, isn't he?*
A: *No, he isn't. He's from Sri Lanka.*

TEST YOURSELF ✔

Close your book. Think of a famous person and 6 things you think you know about him or her. Write 6 tag questions about the person. Then test your classmates' knowledge.

---

1 Learn to offer and respond to help

STUDENT
AUDIO **A** **Look at the picture. Listen to the conversation. Then answer the questions below with your classmates.**

1. What does Abby want to do?
2. What two things does Leo suggest?

STUDENT
AUDIO **B** **Listen and read. What does Abby need help with?**

Leo: You're not still having trouble with your landlord, are you?

Abby: Yes, I am. He hasn't done *any* repairs. I've emailed five times!

Leo: Then it's about time* you got some help. Can I make a suggestion?

Abby: Please do.

Leo: Why don't you do an Internet search on renters' rights?

Abby: OK, but I'll need some help. Could you show me how?

Leo: Sure. Go to a search page and click in the search box. Then type *renters' rights* and our state.

Abby: Then I click *Go*, right?

Leo: Yep, that's it. Look, there are hundreds of renters' rights websites.

Abby: Great! This is really helpful. Thanks so much.

> **In other words...**
>
> **Offering help**
> Can I make a suggestion?
> Can I offer a suggestion?
> Can I suggest something?

*__Idiom note:__ It's about time = It's time for this to happen; it should have happened already

C **Role-play a conversation about help with a partner. Use the example in 1B to make a new conversation.**

Partner A: Ask if your partner is still having trouble with his/her lease. Suggest using an online dictionary to look up difficult words. Help your partner go to the web page and click in the search box. Point out that you can also click on *listen* to hear the word.

Partner B: You've read your lease for a new apartment five times. It has a lot of difficult words, like *premises*. Listen to your partner's suggestions and follow his/her instructions. Check to see if you should click on *search*. Thank your partner.

2 Learn to use question words for clarification

A Study the chart. Complete the questions below with *what* or *where*.

Question words for clarification	
A: I need information on renters' rights. **B:** On **what**? **A:** On renters' rights.	**A:** Click in the search box. **B:** Click **where**? **A:** In the search box.

1. **A:** The states are on a pull-down menu.

   B: On a _____?

2. **A:** Type the URL in the URL box.

   B: Type the URL _____?

B Work with a partner. Match each sentence with a clarification question.

_e_ 1. Click this link first.   a. The what?

____ 2. This link. Then read the FAQs.   b. Ask Tim what?

____ 3. FAQs. There are about ten questions.   c. From where?

____ 4. Ten. They're by a renters' group from Ohio. d. With what?

____ 5. Ohio. You can email them with questions.   e. Click what?

____ 6. Uh... Why don't you ask Tim to help you?   f. About how many?

C Work with a partner. Read the sentences and questions from 2B.

3 Practice your pronunciation

A Listen to the questions. Notice how the speakers use falling and rising intonation.

Falling intonation	Rising intonation
The speaker is fairly sure of the answer.	The speaker is not sure of the answer.
This is a good website, isn't it? ↘	This is a good website, isn't it? ↗
You don't use email often, do you? ↘	You don't use email often, do you? ↗

B Listen. How sure are the speakers of their answers? Check *Fairly sure* or *Not sure*.

	Fairly sure	Not sure
1.		✔
2.		
3.		

	Fairly sure	Not sure
4.		
5.		
6.		

C Practice the questions in 3A with a partner.

4 Focus on listening

A **Talk about the questions with your class.**

1. What are some ways that people find new homes to rent or buy?
2. In your opinion, is it a good idea to look for a home on the Internet? Why or why not?

B **Listen to the interview. Answer the questions.**

1. What are the people talking about?
2. Which person sometimes doesn't speak clearly?

C **Listen again. Complete the sentences.**

1. Melia worked at an apartment rental office in _college_.
2. She learned that most people want to know about the _____'s responsibilities.
3. Melia doesn't think it's _____ to learn to design a website.
4. It took Melia about _____ months to design ApartmentSearch.apt.
5. Larry thinks that _____ people use Melia's site.
6. Melia says that _____ of people visit the site every day.

5 Real-life math

Look at the web page counter and answer the question. Explain your answer to your classmates.

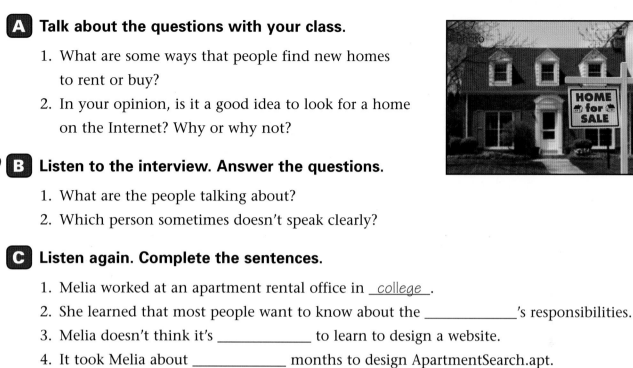

Visitors today: 6 2 5 [ ] [ ] [ ]

Visitors last year: 1 4 9 6 5 0

Today was an unusual day for ApartmentSearch.apt. The website gets about the same number of visitors, or hits, every day. Today was a very busy day. How many more hits did the site get today than it usually gets in a day? _____ (Hint: There are 365 days in a year.)

TEST YOURSELF ✔

Role-play a conversation about using the Internet. Partner A: You want to buy renter's insurance, but you can't find information about it on your insurance company's website. Partner B: Suggest that your friend look at the website's FAQs for information about renter's insurance. Then change roles.

1 Get ready to read

A What are some issues that landlords and renters might disagree about?

B Read the definitions. What is the opposite of *routine*?

check up on: (verb) to look at or visit something to determine its condition
routine: (adj.) normal; usual
tenant: (noun) a renter, a person who pays rent to live in a building

C Look at the title, headings, and pictures in the web article in 2A. Write 2 questions you think the article will answer.

2 Read and respond

A Read the article. How does the law protect renters?

Internet Search _ □ x

Address http://www.renthelp.help ▼ Go

Renters' Helpline: Landlord-Tenant Relations

Are you having problems with your landlord? Check our website! Learn all about your rights and responsibilities as a renter. Housing laws vary from state to state, so be sure to check the laws for your state. Click here to see information for your state.

Your Right to Privacy

Generally, when a landlord needs to enter your home to make routine repairs, he or she must tell you in advance (usually 24 to 48 hours). However, in an emergency, the landlord may enter without advance notice. Check your lease carefully. Local laws vary on whether a landlord may enter your home just to check up on the property.

Your Right to Home Maintenance and Repairs

Landlords are responsible for keeping their properties[1] in good condition. That includes rental units, stairways, and common areas (yards and halls). Landlords must maintain the heating and plumbing systems, supply

[1]properties: buildings or land that a person owns

hot and cold water, and maintain working smoke detectors. Tenants are responsible for keeping their areas clean.

Your Right to Your Security Deposit

The landlord must refund your security deposit when you move out if there is no damage to the apartment. Before you move in, it's a good idea to use a checklist to note the condition of everything in the home, including plumbing, appliances, and locks. Give a copy to your landlord and keep a copy. You may need it if your landlord tries to keep some of your security deposit when you move out.

Source: *www.jud2.ct.gov*

B **Listen and read the article again.**

C **Choose the best answers. Circle *a* or *b*.**

1. What is the most important idea in the first section of the article?
   a. A landlord can enter your home at any time.
   b. A landlord can only enter your home in certain situations.

2. What is the most important idea in the last section of the article?
   a. The law protects renters' security deposits.
   b. The renter has to pay for any damage to an apartment.

3. What is the main idea of the article?
   a. Landlords have more rights than renters do.
   b. Renters have rights under the law.

D **Look at the questions you wrote in 1C. Did the article answer the questions?**

3 Talk it over

Think about the questions. Talk about your ideas with the class.

1. What are some ways that landlords and tenants can have a good relationship?
2. How can the Internet help renters and home buyers?

> **BRING IT TO LIFE**
>
> Use the Internet or the library to find a checklist of things to look at in choosing an apartment or a house. Bring your information to class. Compare checklists with a group. With your group, list the top ten things to ask or do when renting a home.

1 Grammar

A Circle the correct tags.

1. This apartment is nice, (doesn't it / (isn't it))?
2. We looked at apartments in this building last year, (didn't we / don't we)?
3. The building was built a long time ago, (didn't it / wasn't it)?
4. The halls and stairways are pretty clean, (aren't they / are they)?
5. The landlord doesn't allow pets, (do they / does he)?
6. You know some people who live here, (do you / don't you)?

B Complete the sentences with tag questions with a form of *be* or *do*.

1. This is the same website we looked at yesterday, _____isn't it_____?
2. The cursor moves when you move the mouse, _____?
3. Some of these links don't work anymore, _____?
4. We're going to print this page, _____?
5. You didn't click on that pop-up ad, _____?
6. This information wasn't here the last time we checked this site, _____?

C Match the sentences with the clarification questions.

_c_ 1. I found a website with free email.	a. Is where?
___ 2. We could email the building supervisor.	b. Since when?
___ 3. We need to tell him about our sink.	c. With what?
___ 4. It's been broken since last week.	d. Email who?
___ 5. The sink is in the kitchen.	e. Our what?

D You want to move into a new apartment. Write questions with tags for these situations.

1. You think you have to write a letter to your current landlord.

    I have to write a letter to my current landlord, don't I?

2. You think your current landlord is going to give back your security deposit.

    _____

3. You're not sure, but you think that the new building doesn't have cable TV.

    _____

4. You're fairly certain that the rent for the new apartment includes utilities.

    _____

2 Group work

A Work with 2–3 classmates. Write a 6–8 line conversation between the people in the picture. Share your conversation with the class.

A: *You're good with computers, aren't you?*
  I need some help finding...
B: *I can help you...*

B Choose one of the questions below. Interview 3 classmates. Write their answers.

1. Are computers and technology important to you? Why or why not?
2. Should public libraries use their budgets to buy books or to provide computers? Why?
3. Some people spend most of their time using the Internet. Is this a problem? Why or why not?

C Talk about the answers with your class.

PROBLEM SOLVING

 A Listen and read about Eric.

Eric doesn't know how to use a computer very well. Everyone in his family is good with computers, and Eric would like to be able to use email and find information on the Internet.

Eric's brother, Louis, is a computer expert. Louis has offered to help Eric learn to use the Internet, but it's difficult for Eric to learn from his brother. Louis talks quickly, and he likes to show Eric how to do things instead of letting Eric try for himself. Eric finds it really hard to learn that way. Eric likes having his brother's help, but so far, he hasn't learned anything.

B Work with your classmates. Answer the questions.

1. What is Eric's problem?
2. What could he do? Think of 2 or 3 solutions to Eric's problem.
3. Write a conversation between Eric and his brother.

UNIT **12**

How did I do?

FOCUS ON
• achievements and leadership
• personal goals and plans
• gerunds as objects
• giving and getting feedback
• success stories

LESSON 1 **Vocabulary**

1 Learn achievement vocabulary

A **Talk about the questions with your class.**

1. What is something you've done that you're really proud of?
2. What is something you'd like to achieve in your life?

B **Work with your classmates. Match the words with the pictures.**

_____ achieve a goal   ⎯1⎯ have a dream   _____ start a business

_____ give back to the community   _____ overcome adversity   _____ win a scholarship

C **Listen and check. Then read the new words with a partner.**

D **Work with a partner. Write other achievement words you know.**
Check your words in a dictionary.

E Work with a partner. Talk about these questions. Use the words in 1B.

1. What things did Elio do before he achieved his goal?
2. Why do you think Elio wanted to give back to the community?

2 Learn vocabulary for leadership qualities

A Look at the checklist. Check the words that describe you.

DESCRIBE YOUR LEADERSHIP QUALITIES

ARE YOU A LEADER?

Check (✔) the boxes that describe you.

	IS THIS YOU?	THEN YOU...
☐	**Confident**	are usually sure of what you are doing, and that your ideas are good.
☐	**Courageous**	don't mind trying something difficult or even a little scary.
☐	**Assertive**	aren't afraid to say what you think, but you do it politely.
☐	**Dedicated**	believe in what you are doing, and you work hard.
☐	**Practical**	are realistic. You know what's possible and what isn't.
☐	**Competent**	are good at what you do.

B Work with a partner. Practice the conversation. Use the words in 2A.

A: *Which leadership qualities do you think you have?*
B: *Well, I'm not afraid to say what I think, so I guess I'm pretty assertive. What about you?*
A: *I'm really dedicated. I believe in what I'm doing.*

C Talk about the questions with your class.

1. Talk about someone you know who has achieved something important. What did the person do before he or she achieved the goal?
2. Talk about someone you know who has good leadership qualities. Which qualities does the person have? How do you know?

TEST YOURSELF ✔

Close your book. Categorize the new words in two lists: *Goals and Achievements* and *Leadership Qualities*. Check your spelling in a dictionary. Compare your lists with a partner.

LESSON 2 Real-life writing

1 Read an application essay

A Talk about the questions with your class.

1. What are some situations when it's OK to talk about your achievements? What are some situations when it's not OK? Why?

2. Do you like to talk about your plans for the future? Why or why not?

 B Listen and read the essay.

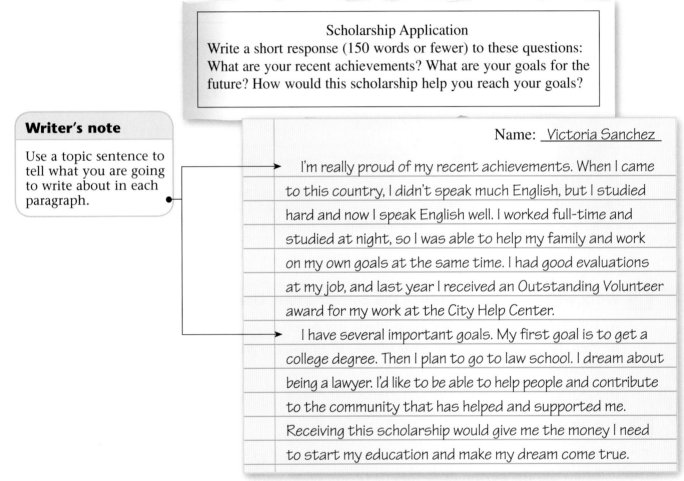

Scholarship Application
Write a short response (150 words or fewer) to these questions:
What are your recent achievements? What are your goals for the future? How would this scholarship help you reach your goals?

Writer's note

Use a topic sentence to tell what you are going to write about in each paragraph.

Name: _Victoria Sanchez_

I'm really proud of my recent achievements. When I came to this country, I didn't speak much English, but I studied hard and now I speak English well. I worked full-time and studied at night, so I was able to help my family and work on my own goals at the same time. I had good evaluations at my job, and last year I received an Outstanding Volunteer award for my work at the City Help Center.

I have several important goals. My first goal is to get a college degree. Then I plan to go to law school. I dream about being a lawyer. I'd like to be able to help people and contribute to the community that has helped and supported me. Receiving this scholarship would give me the money I need to start my education and make my dream come true.

C Check your understanding. Work with a partner. Ask and answer the questions.

1. What did Victoria choose to say in her topic sentences? Why?
2. Why did she list both school and non-school achievements?
3. What goals did she list?
4. Did she answer all of the questions in the application?
5. How many words did she use? Was she within the limit?

2 Write an application essay

A **Talk about the questions with your class.**

    1. Why do people usually apply for scholarships?

    2. What kinds of achievements help people get scholarships and other awards?

B **Write a short essay about your achievements and goals for a scholarship application. Use the model in 1B and the questions below to help you.**

Paragraph 1: How do you feel about your recent achievements? (your topic sentence)

            What are your recent achievements?

            What did you do to achieve these things?

Paragraph 2: How many goals do you have for the future? (your topic sentence)

            What are your goals and plans for the future?

            How will this scholarship help you reach your goals?

> Scholarship Application
> Write a short response (150 words or fewer) to these questions:
> What are your recent achievements? What are your goals for
> the future? How would this scholarship help you achieve your
>
> Name: _____
>
> I'm really proud of my recent achievements...
>
> I have several goals for the future...

C **Use the checklist to edit your writing. Check (✔) the true sentences.**

Editing checklist	
1. My topic sentences tell what I am going to write about.	
2. In the first paragraph, I wrote about my achievements.	
3. In the second paragraph, I wrote about my goals.	
4. My essay is not more than 150 words.	

D **Exchange essays with a partner. Read and comment on your partner's work.**

    1. Point out one sentence that you think will help your partner get a scholarship.

    2. Ask your partner about his or her achievements and goals.

TEST YOURSELF ✔

Write a new essay to recommend your partner for a scholarship. Talk about your
partner's achievements and goals and why your partner should receive the scholarship.

LESSON **3** Grammar

1 Learn to use gerunds after prepositions

A Read the performance review. What is Kim Tran's job title?

S&S hotels

PERFORMANCE REVIEW

Name <u>Kim Tran</u>   Title <u>Desk Clerk</u>   Reviewing Manager <u>M. Perez</u>

Period of Review <u>9/06 - 9/07</u>   Date of Review <u>10/15/07</u>

Rating Codes: *E = excellent   S = satisfactory   NI = needs improvement*

Responsibility	Rating	Comments
Greets hotel guests, answers questions and requests	E	Ms. Tran does a good job of welcoming guests. She cares about helping people.
Records information accurately	S	She checks information after recording it.
Takes phone messages	NI	She needs to work on taking messages.

B Study the chart. Circle the 4 examples of gerunds after prepositions in 1A.

GERUNDS AFTER PREPOSITIONS

Preposition + gerund
She does a good job **of welcoming** guests.
She knows a lot **about managing** the front desk.
Instead **of getting** a promotion, she got a raise.
She needs to work **on taking** messages.

Notes
• Gerunds are used after prepositions like *about, at, for, in, of,* and *to*.
• Gerunds are also used after verb phrases with prepositions: She cares about **helping** people.

C Complete the sentences in Kim's review. Use gerunds.

Kim does a good job of _____greeting_____ guests and _____ them about
1. greet   2. ask

their stay when they check out. Before _____ me about problems, she tries
3. call

to solve them herself. Kim often works late hours without _____. Instead of
4. complain

_____ down when the desk isn't busy, she helps out by _____ for
5. sit   6. look

extra work to do. Her work contributes to _____ the hotel more welcoming for
7. make

our guests.

☑ Use gerunds after prepositions to interpret evaluations and feedback

D **Match the parts of the sentences.**

_b_ 1. Kim cares about   a. helping employees.

____ 2. She sometimes worries about   b. doing her job well.

____ 3. The hotel managers believe in   c. remembering people's names.

____ 4. Kim looks forward to   d. learning more about the hotel business.

2 Learn gerunds after *be* + adjective + preposition

A **Study the chart. What verb is used in all of these sentences?**

Be + adjective + preposition + gerund
The manager **is responsible for evaluating** Kim's work.
Kim **was happy about getting** a raise.
The guests **were interested in hearing** about the hotel's services.

Note
Certain adjectives are almost always followed by a preposition. For example, *interested* is usually followed by *in*:   She's interested in taking a management class.

B **Look at the adjectives + prepositions in the box. Complete the sentences. Then compare answers with a partner.**

nervous about   tired of   ~~good at~~   proud of   interested in

1. **A:** Is your boss _____good at_____ giving helpful feedback?

   B: No. My boss marks everyone "Needs Improvement."

2. **A:** I'm really _____ being evaluated next week.

   Reviews make my stomach hurt.

   B: Don't worry. Your boss is only _____ helping you.

   That's what feedback is for.

3. **A:** Aren't you _____ doing the same work every day?

   B: Not really. I'm _____ being good at what I do.

C **Write your answers. Then ask and answer the questions with a partner.**

1. What are you interested in learning?

2. What are you afraid of doing?

3. What do you believe in doing?

3 Grammar listening

 Listen to the people talk about Michael. Choose the sentences with the same meaning. Circle *a* or *b*.

1. a. He might try a new career.
   b. He tried a new career.

2. a. He's tired all the time.
   b. He doesn't like his job.

3. a. He'll start a new business.
   b. He'll stay with the company.

4. a. He's spent his money.
   b. He's saved his money.

5. a. His job makes him nervous.
   b. The change makes him nervous.

6. a. He'll make a decision.
   b. He's made a decision.

4 Practice gerunds after prepositions

A **Think about your answers to these questions.**

1. What are you good at doing?
2. What is one thing you have been thinking about doing but have never done?
3. What is one thing you are tired of doing every day?
4. What are you planning on doing in the future?
5. What's one change you plan on making in the next five years?

B **Work with a partner. Ask and answer the questions.**

A: *What are you good at doing?*
B: *Well, I'm pretty good at...*

C **Talk about your partner with the class.**

Ernestine is good at...

> **TEST YOURSELF** ✔
> Close your book. Write 6 sentences about yourself and your partner.
> Use the information from 4A and 4B. Use a gerund after a preposition
> in each sentence.

1 Learn to participate in a performance review

STUDENT AUDIO **A** Look at the picture. Listen to the conversation. Then answer the questions below with your classmates.

1. What positive feedback does Kim hear?
2. What negative feedback does she hear?

STUDENT AUDIO **B** Listen and read. What does Kim's supervisor want her to do?

A: Well, Kim, you've done pretty well this past year.

B: Thank you.

A: You've done a great job of helping guests, and you've started making suggestions, too. I really value that.

B: I appreciate your saying so.

A: I'd like to see some improvement, though, in the way you deal with* phone messages. Sometimes your co-workers can't understand the phone messages you write.

B: Oh, I'm sorry. I didn't know there was a problem. Can you tell me what I need to do?

A: I'd suggest asking the caller about anything you don't understand.

B: I see. I'll try to do better.

A: That would be great.

*Idiom note:** deal with = take care of

> **In other words...**
>
> **Responding to feedback**
>
> I appreciate your saying so.
>
> I didn't know there was a problem.
>
> Thanks for saying so.
>
> I didn't realize anything was wrong.

C Role-play a performance review with a partner. Use the example in 1B to make a new conversation.

Partner A: You're the manager of a clothing store. Go over your employee's performance review. Your employee keeps the store neat and handles money well. You'd like to see some improvement in his or her customer service. Sometimes the employee avoids talking to customers. Tell your employee to offer to help customers when they walk in the door.

Partner B: You're an employee at a clothing store. Listen and respond to the manager's positive feedback. Listen to the manager's negative feedback and ask for advice. Promise to do better.

2 Learn polite requests and suggestions with gerunds

A Study the chart. What two phrases can you use to make polite requests and suggestions in question form?

Polite requests and suggestions with gerunds
I would suggest delivering messages right away.
I'd recommend taking a training class.
May I suggest getting an earlier bus?
Would you mind telling me a little more about the opportunity?

B Work with a partner. Write polite requests or suggestions. Use each polite expression in 2A once.

1. Can I give you some advice? Apply for a management position.

   May I suggest applying for a management position?

2. Give me some more information.

   _____

3. Think about your long-term goals.

   _____

4. Make a plan to reach your goals.

   _____

C Work with a partner. Read the actions in the box. Which things should you avoid doing at a performance review? Which would you recommend doing?

argue   listen carefully   talk a lot   criticize co-workers   ask for suggestions

I'd avoid arguing with my supervisor. I'd recommend...

3 Practice your pronunciation

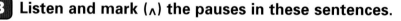

A Listen to the sentences. Notice how the words are grouped. (∧ = pause)

1. I'd suggest asking the caller ∧ about anything you don't understand.
2. I was able to help my family ∧ and work on my own goals ∧ at the same time.

B Listen and mark (∧) the pauses in these sentences.

1. I'd like to see some changes ∧ in the way you deal with phone messages.
2. Is a training class for cooks something you'd be interested in?
3. She helps out her co-workers by looking for extra work to do.
4. I've learned a lot about working in a restaurant kitchen since I got this job.

C Practice the sentences in 3A and 3B with a partner.

4 Focus on listening

A Talk about the questions with your class.

1. What are three things an employer can say to give positive feedback?
2. What are three ways an employer can introduce negative feedback?

B Listen to the speakers. Do the managers use positive feedback or negative feedback with the employees? Check (✔) *Positive feedback* or *Negative feedback*.

	Positive feedback	Negative feedback			Positive feedback	Negative feedback
1.		✔		4.		
2.				5.		
3.				6.		

C Listen again. Choose the best response. Circle *a* or *b*.

1. a. Thank you. I will.
   b. I'm really sorry.

2. a. Thanks. That's good to hear.
   b. I didn't know anything was wrong.

3. a. I appreciate your saying so.
   b. I'll try to do better.

4. a. I'm sorry, but I can't.
   b. I'm sorry.

5. a. Yes, I do.
   b. I didn't know there was a problem.

6. a I didn't know anything was wrong.
   b. That's wonderful. Thank you.

5 Real-life math

A Survey the class. Ask the following question.

Are you most interested in having a career that you love, making a lot of money, or having a lot of free time?

B Write the totals for each response on the board. Figure out the percentage for each answer. Then make a pie chart to show your classmates' opinions.

There are 20 students in our class. Five students are most interested in making a lot of money. That's 25%.

> **TEST YOURSELF** ✔
> Role-play a classroom conversation. Partner A: You're an ESL teacher. Talk to a student.
> Tell the student two things he or she does well and one thing that needs work.
> Partner B: Listen and respond to the teacher's feedback. Then change roles.

1 Get ready to read

A Do you think there are jobs that only men, or only women, should do? Explain your answer.

B Read the definitions. What is one traditional thing that you do?

eventually: (adv.) after a long time
gradually: (adv.) slowly
tradition: (noun) something people in a culture have done for a long time

C Look at the title and the picture in the newspaper article in 2A. Write a question you think the article will answer.

2 Read and respond

A Read the article. What has Ms. Sugimoto achieved?

Eri Sugimoto's Story

Historically and traditionally, making sushi, the Japanese rice-and-raw-fish favorite, has always been a man's world. Some people believed that women's hands were too warm to make sushi. Today, however, the number of female sushi chefs in the U.S., and in Japan, is gradually starting to rise.

When Eri Sugimoto was in her early 20s, she worked as a cook at a restaurant in Tokyo, cooking home-style Japanese food. Over time, she became interested in learning to make sushi. "I have always wanted to work with raw fish because I love to eat it," said Ms. Sugimoto. However, she knew of only one sushi chef who was a woman.

She asked a friend who owned several sushi restaurants if she could apprentice[1] with one of his chefs. "I had to beg him to let me clean the restaurant," Ms. Sugimoto said. He said "yes," so she mopped floors, waited on tables, and learned to make sushi. She bought fish with her own money and practiced making sushi for hours at home. It took her a year just to make the rice correctly. Eventually, she learned to make fifty kinds of sushi, but she had to practice for two years before being allowed to serve her sushi to customers.

In 2000, Ms. Sugimoto finally began working at a sushi restaurant in New York City. She became the restaurant's only female sushi chef. The restaurant's owner said, "It's time to break tradition. Why not women chefs?"

Ms. Sugimoto's achievement has opened the door for others to reach their dreams.

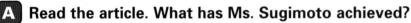

[1] apprentice: learn a skill from an expert by working for him or her

Copyright © 2002 by the New York Times Co. Adapted from "She Has a Knife and She Knows How to Use It" by Elaine Louie, originally published June 5, 2002, by the New York Times

✔ Read and interpret a newspaper article about a personal achievement

B Listen and read the article again.

C In what order did these events happen in Ms. Sugimoto's life? Number the events from 1 (first) to 5 (last).

_____ 1. She served sushi to customers.

_____ 2. She became interested in making sushi.

_____ 3. She became a sushi chef at a restaurant in New York.

_____ 4. She apprenticed with a sushi chef.

_1_ 5. She worked at a restaurant in Tokyo.

D Study the chart. Complete the sentences below with compound adjectives from the chart.

> **Word Study: Using hyphens to make compound adjectives**
>
> Sometimes two or more words are joined together by a hyphen (-) to show that they make one compund adjective.
>
> | Words | Compound Adjective |
> | --- | --- |
> | home style | home-style restaurant |
> | long term | long-term plans |
> | real life | real-life math |
> | sushi making | sushi-making class |

1. Ms. Sugimoto's __long-term__ goal was to learn to make sushi.

2. She was the only _____ apprentice who was a woman.

3. Before that, she had worked in a restaurant doing _____ cooking.

4. Today, hers is a _____ success story.

3 Talk it over

Think about the questions. Talk about your ideas with the class.

1. How can the success of a person like Ms. Sugimoto help other people?

2. People often use the phrase "the good old days" to say that life was better in the past. What do you think about "the good old days"? Were they better? Why or why not?

BRING IT TO LIFE

Use the public library or the Internet to find an article with a short biography (life story) of an interesting person. Bring the biography to class and talk about the person's achievements with your group.

1 Grammar

A Complete the sentences. Use the gerund form or the simple present of the verbs in parentheses.

1. Alfredo doesn't believe in ____talking____ about his achievements. He never ____talks____ about them. (talk)

2. He _____ at the Literacy Center. He got an award for _____ to help people learn to read. (volunteer)

3. He never _____ down for long. He stays busy instead of _____ on the couch and watching TV. (sit)

4. Alfredo cares about _____ people. He always _____ me. (help)

B Complete the sentences with adjectives from the box.

good	interested	nervous	proud	~~responsible~~	tired

1. At work, I'm _responsible_ for taking care of the youngest children.

2. At first, I wasn't very _____ at talking to the parents.

3. Sometimes I think my family is _____ of hearing me talk about the children.

4. I'm happy with my work. I am _____ of doing a good job with the children.

5. I'm _____ about getting my first performance review tomorrow. I'm _____ in hearing the director's feedback.

C Complete the email. Use the verbs in parentheses.

📧 **Email - Message (Plain Text)** — □ ×

File   Edit   View   Insert   Format   Tools   Actions   Help

Reply | Reply to All | Forward | Print | Save | Delete | Previous | Next

Hi Alex,

Would you ___mind answering___ a couple of questions about my college applications? What
   1. (mind, answer)

standardized tests do you _____? Would you _____ my
     2. (recommend, take)   3. (suggest, send)

grades to the colleges I'm interested in? How many colleges do you _____ to?
             4. (recommend, apply)

Thanks so much. I really appreciate your help.

Ted

2 Group work

A Work with 2–3 classmates. Write a 6–8 line conversation between the people in the picture. Share your conversation with the class.

A: *You've done very well over the last six months.*
B: *Thank you...*

B Interview 3 classmates. Write their answers.

1. Name someone you think is really successful. What has that person achieved?
2. What is one achievement of yours that your classmates probably don't know about?
3. Name one leadership quality that you would like to work on developing. Why did you choose this quality?

C Talk about the answers with your class.

PROBLEM SOLVING

A Listen and read about Jafari.

When Jafari immigrated to the U.S. ten years ago, he had a lot of dreams. Life wasn't easy at first. He worked two jobs and didn't have much time to work on his goals. But over time, things got easier. Jafari was able to go to college, find a good job, and finally buy a house for his family.

Today, Jafari owns his own business and is proud of everything he's accomplished. Now that he has a little more free time, he's interested in giving something back to the community. He'd like to be involved in something that would really make his community a better place to live, but he doesn't know where to start.

B Work with your classmates. Answer the questions.

1. What is Jafari's problem?
2. What should he do? Think of 2 or 3 possible solutions for Jafari.
3. Write a short letter to Jafari. Tell him what you think he should do.

LISTENING SCRIPT

UNIT 1: It Takes All Kinds!

Pg. 4 Lesson 1—Exercise 1C

W = Woman, N = Narrator
1. W: My new class is great. There are some really interesting people in it. Let me tell you something about them. That's Omar. He likes to talk, and he likes words. If you don't know what a word means, just ask Omar! He's a verbal person.
   N: verbal
2. W: Fatima's good with numbers, and she's good at solving problems. She wants to teach math someday. She's very mathematical.
   N: mathematical
3. W: Now that's Ari. On the weekends, he goes canoeing or climbs mountains. He loves going to new places and trying new things. He's adventurous.
   N: adventurous
4. W: Nora likes spending time with people. She's so friendly; everyone likes her. I'd definitely say she's social.
   N: social
5. W: That's Ariana. She paints pictures. She loves to work with her hands. She's very artistic.
   N: artistic
6. W: That's Carlos. He plays the guitar and the piano. He's really musical.
   N: musical
7. W: Eric likes to run, play basketball, and swim. If it's a sport, he likes it. He plays soccer on the weekends. He's athletic.
   N: athletic
8. W: And that's me. I don't talk a lot in class, but I really like listening to what other people say. I guess I'm pretty quiet.
   N: quiet

Pg. 10 Lesson 3—Exercise 3

1. Eric is a lot like his brother, Tom. He looks like him. They both have black eyes and dark hair. And they like the same things.
2. Omar reads a book every week. Then he writes a report about it. He also makes lists of the new words he learns when he reads.
3. Ariana doesn't have a car. She doesn't really need one. But she wants a new bicycle. She believes that bicycles are good for the environment.
4. Nora and her sister go to the community center every Saturday. They swim in the pool there and talk with their friends.
5. Ari, the adventurous one, climbs mountains and travels to far-away places. He does something new every time he takes a vacation.
6. Some people think that I'm not very social, but that's not true. I may seem unfriendly, but I really like people. I also like to be alone sometimes. My friends understand that about me.

Pg. 11 Lesson 4—Exercise 1A

W = Woman, M = Man
1. W: I think our school is great. What's your opinion?
   M: Well, I think the teachers are great and the campus is nice, but my classes always have too many students.
   W: Really? Do you prefer smaller classes?
   M: Yes, I love small classes! I think they're better for students.
   W: Maybe you're right, but in a large class you can meet lots of people. I like that.
2. M: I think teachers should get more money.
   W: That may be so, but their job seems easy.
   M: Easy? Really? Why do you say that?
   W: Because they just talk to students all day. That's not very difficult.
   M: I'm not sure I agree. I think teaching is hard work.

Pg. 13 Lesson 4—Exercise 4B

T = Talk show host, K= Dr. Kwang, H = Mr. Holt
T: Our guests today are Dr. Violet Kwang, from the Center for Education, and Mr. Fred Holt, from Hills County Public Schools. Welcome to you both.
K: Thank you.
H: Thanks.
T: Let's start with a general question. What would you say is the biggest problem facing our schools today?
K: Well, for me, it's a problem of staffing. We simply don't have enough good teachers.
H: I would have to agree. We need to get more college graduates to become teachers.
T: And how can we do that?
K: By paying teachers higher salaries and giving them better benefits.
H: I agree totally.
K: And with more teachers, we could have smaller classes. Right now, there are too many students in most classes.
H: But then we'd need more schools— or at least more classrooms.
K: We need to build new schools. There's no question about that.
H: I'm not sure I agree. Where is the money for new schools going to come from?
K: From taxes. We need just a small increase in state taxes.
H: I have to disagree on that one, too. Nobody wants higher taxes.
T: OK. Well, what about safety in our schools? Are things getting any better?
H: We think so. And we hope to install security cameras in every high school next year. That should help a lot.
K: Security cameras? That doesn't sound like a very good idea. The money you're going to spend on cameras needs to go toward new books and computers.
H: I agree that we need books and computers, but safety is important, too.

T: Well, we're out of time. Thank you both for being here. See you next time on *The Education Show*. Bye!

UNIT 2: Keeping Current

Pg. 18 Lesson 1—Exercise 1C

W = Wanda, S = Stan, N = Narrator
1. W: Good morning, Stan. Hey, did you see the *Times* this morning? There was a great article about the meeting of world leaders on the front page.
   N: front page
2. S: Uh…, well, I don't have much time in the morning.
   W: Hmmm, that's too bad. It's interesting to find out people's opinions of the news and politics. At least you should take the time to read the editorial page.
   N: editorial page
3. S: OK, OK, Wanda! Sometimes I read more of the paper. When I was looking for a job and a good used car, I always checked the classified ads.
   N: classified ads
4. S: And come to think of it, I've learned a lot about things around the home, exercising, and healthy eating in the lifestyle section.
   N: lifestyle section
5. W: Well, yes, the newspaper is useful for that kind of thing, too. If I want to see movie or a TV show, I look at the entertainment section.
   N: entertainment section
6. S: Yes, and any time I miss a baseball or football game on TV, I read the sports section.
   N: sports section
   W: Still Stan—it's a newspaper—you should take a look at the news once in a while.
   S: OK, Wanda, OK… (sound of crinkling newspaper) Happy now?

Pg. 24 Lesson 3—Exercise 3

1. Our car was hit by a tree.
2. The information was given to the reporter by the neighbors.
3. The teenagers' parents were called by the police.
4. The fire was caused by an electrical problem.

Pg. 25 Lesson 4—Exercise 1A

W = Woman, M = Man
W: Did you hear about the protest downtown?
M: No. What was it about?
W: The city wanted to prohibit food carts on the street. You know, those carts that sell sodas and snacks downtown. The protesters tied themselves to the carts.
M: The city wanted to limit the carts?
W: No, not limit, they wanted to *prohibit* them. They didn't want *any* carts in the city. The protesters were very upset.
M: I can understand that. We need to support small businesses—and the food is good and cheap. So were the carts prohibited?
W: No. To make a long story short, the protesters won. The carts were allowed to stay.

Pg. 27 Lesson 4—Exercise 4B

Thousands of people were told to leave their homes today in Florida towns along the Gulf Coast. Weather forecasters predict Hurricane Timothy will reach the coast sometime Wednesday. Local residents must leave their homes by noon today. Several schools in neighboring towns were opened for the residents to stay in. Food and water are being brought in. The hurricane is expected to bring strong winds and heavy rain. Because of the dangerous conditions, news reporters, including myself, were also asked to leave by local officials. From the Florida Gulf Coast, this is Ron Avery, reporting live for Channel 4 News.

UNIT 3: Going Places

Pg. 32 Lesson 1—Exercise 1C

W1 = Woman 1, M1 = Man 1, N = Narrator, O = Operator, M2 = Man 2, W2 = Woman 2, B = Bus Driver, D = Dispatch Operator, W3 = Woman 3, M3 = Man 3
1. W1: Gary, what's that sound? Look at the smoke coming out from the hood.
   M1: Oh no! I can't believe this. Another problem with this car? We don't have time to have a breakdown.
   N: have a breakdown
2. W1: Turn on the hazard lights—we need to warn other drivers.
   M1: I already did. I know it's important to turn on the hazard lights.
   N: turn on the hazard lights
3. W1: I'll call the auto club. They'll help us.
   O: Thank you for calling All City Auto Club. May I help you?
   W1: My husband didn't want to call you, but I did… our engine was smoking, and now we're on the side of the road, across from the city mall. I told my husband we had to call the auto club.
   N: call the auto club
4. O: OK. If the smoke is gone, he can raise the hood of the car.
   W1: If there's no more smoke, the operator says to raise the hood of the car.
   N: raise the hood

5. M2: Oh, great! We've got a flat tire.
   W2: We're miles from a gas station. This is a terrible place to have a flat tire.
   N: have a flat tire
6. W2: Honey, do you need help changing the tire?
   M2: I'm OK. Just keep the kids away. It's not that hard to change a tire.
   N: change a tire

7. B: Oh, this is bad. The bus breaks down on my first day of work. OK, first thing to do is use these safety triangles…gotta warn the other drivers. Geez, this is a big bus. I've got to use a lot of safety triangles.
   N: use a safety triangle

8. B: Dispatch? This is driver 719. My bus
      broke down at Cedar and King. Can
      you send a tow truck right away?
   D: No problem. We'll send a tow truck.
   N: send a tow truck
9. W3: That's it. I have to walk… Excuse me, I can't
      wait for the bus, and I need to get directions
      to the library from here. Can you help me?
   M3: I'm not from this area, but I believe
      you go straight on this street for two
      blocks, then turn left. The library
      should be on your right. I hope…
   W3: Thanks. And don't worry about it. If I get lost,
      I can call my roommate to get directions.
   N: get directions

Pg. 38   Lesson 3—Exercise 3

W1 = Woman 1, M1 = Man 1, M2 = Man 2,
W2 = Woman 2, M3 = Man 3, W3 = Woman 3,
M4 = Man 4, W4 = Woman 4, W5 = Woman 5,
M5 = Man 5, M6 = Man 6, M7 = Man 7,
W6 = Woman 6, W7 = Woman 7, M8 = Man 8,
M9 = Man 9, W8 = Woman 8
1. W1: Hi, David. What's up?
   M1: I'm lost!
2. M2: Hi, Patricia. Is everything OK?
   W2: No, it isn't. I have a flat tire.
3. M3: Hi, Gina. How are you?
   W3: Not so good. My car broke down.
      I'm waiting for a tow truck.
4. M4: Hi Donna. It's Sam. I'm with Joe.
   W4: It's late. Where are you guys?
   M4: We're stuck in traffic.
5. W5: Do you want to drive with me?
   M5: No. I'm taking the bus.
   M6: Yeah. I'm taking the bus, too.
6. M7: Cindy, why don't you call your sister?
      She can help.
   W6: I don't have a cell phone.
7. W7: Hi, Hank. What's going on?
   M8: I'm not going to class today.
      My car's out of gas.
8. M9: Do you need anything else
      for your trip, Maria?
   W8: I need a map.

Pg. 39   Lesson 4—Exercise 1A

M = Man, A = Artie, W = Woman, R = Rhonda
1. M: Hey, Artie. I'm thinking about going to
      San Francisco next month. I have a long
      weekend and I've never been there before.
   A: Have you already booked your ticket?
   M: No, but my cousin said to look for
      a ticket on the Internet. Do you
      have any website suggestions?
   A: I'd check out Southair if I were you.
   M: Is it hard to find information on the website?
   A: Nah—it's really easy. And I bet
      they'll have the cheapest prices.
   M: Thanks!
2. W: Rhonda, I'm traveling to Atlanta next month,
      but I don't know anything about the city.
   R: Do you have your hotel reservation?
   W: Not yet. I don't know any motels in that
      city. Can you give me a recommendation?

R: You could stay in a Motel 22. They're all over
   the U.S. They probably have a motel in Atlanta.
W: Is it hard to find out?
R: No, it's easy. Just call their 800
   number and make a reservation.
W: That's a great idea. Thanks for your help.
R: My pleasure.

Pg. 41   Lesson 4—Exercise 4B

Welcome to the Motel 22 automated message
system. Please listen to the following choices.
To make a room reservation at one of our 120
motels around the country, please press one.
To locate the Motel 22 nearest you, please
press 2 and enter your zip code.
To inquire about reserving 15 or more
rooms for a conference, wedding, or
other large event, please press 3.
For employment information, please press 4.
For all other inquiries, please call 1-800-555-5252.
To hear this message again, please press the pound key.
Thank you for calling Motel 22.

UNIT 4:   Get the Job

Pg. 46   Lesson 1—Exercise 1C

W = Woman, N = Narrator
   W: If you're thinking about your future, one
      of the things you really should do is visit
      the career center. It's a great place.
1. W: I'm starting a medical-technician training
      class next week. I needed help to pay for
      my classes, so I applied for financial aid. If
      money for training or college is a problem
      for you, you should apply for financial aid.
   N: apply for financial aid
2. W: A career counselor can help you apply for jobs
      or practice for an interview. I recommend that
      everyone see the career counselor at the center.
   N: see a career counselor
3. W: Our career center has a classroom
      upstairs. It's really convenient to take
      a training class at the center.
   N: take a training class
4. W: The career center posts new jobs on the job
      board every week. That's how my sister found
      her job. It definitely pays to look at job listings.
   N: look at job listings
5. W: And I always use the resource center.
      They have a lot of books about finding
      a good job and planning for a career.
      It's easy to use the resource center.
   N: use the resource center
6. W: In the resource center, you can take an
      interest inventory on the computer. This
      computer program matches your interests to
      different types of jobs. You'll learn a lot about
      yourself if you take an interest inventory.
   N: take an interest inventory

Pg. 52   Lesson 3—Exercise 3

Coming to live in the U.S. meant a lot of
big changes in my life. Everything here was
different. Before I came here, I had never lived

in a small town; I had always lived in a big city. Now, I live in a small town, and I love it.

In my home country, I spoke English, so that's not different. I studied French in school, but since there are a lot of Spanish-speaking people in my neighborhood in the U.S., now I study Spanish.

And I have different goals now. Before I came to the U.S., I had always wanted to be a businessman. Now, I want to be a teacher.

Pg. 53   Lesson 4—Exercise 1A

I = Interviewer, J1 = Job Applicant 1 (Ms. Jones), J2 = Job Applicant 2 (Ms. Adams)
1. I: Tell me about your experience, Ms. Jones.
    J1: You mean work experience?
    I: Yes.
    J1: Well, I've never really had a job.
    I: I see. How about training?
    J1: You mean like job training?
    I: Yes.
    J1: No. I haven't had that, either.
    I: Well, thank you, Ms. Jones.
2. I: Tell me about your experience, Ms. Adams.
    J2: Do you mean work experience?
    I: Yes.
    J2: Well, I've worked in a restaurant for the last two years.
    I: I see. How about training?
    J2: Is that job training?
    I: Yes.
    J2: Well, let's see. I took a class in restaurant cooking at the college. And I've always loved cooking for my family.
    I: I see. That's good. You have a lot of the skills we're looking for.
    J2: Thank you.

Pg. 55   Lesson 4—Exercise 4B

H = Hanna, L = Liz
H: I'm working on my resume, and I have some questions. Could you help me out with a couple of things?
L: Sure. I'd be happy to. What's the problem?
H: Well, I'm taking a training class at the college, but I haven't finished yet. How do I write that?
L: Just write the month you started the class *to present*. That shows you haven't finished yet.
H: Uh-huh. I took an ESL class, too. Should I include that?
L: Yes, definitely. When did you finish?
H: Last year.
L: OK, then just write the school, the place, the name of the class, and the year.
H: And what about high school? I graduated from high school in my country.
L: I think you should include that, too. Write *high school diploma*, and the year you received it.
H: Great. I've already finished the employment history, so I think I'm done. Thanks for your help.
L: My pleasure. Now you just have to type it neatly, and then check it—twice.

UNIT 5:   Safe and Sound

Pg. 60   Lesson 1—Exercise 1C

W = Woman, N = Narrator
1. W: We work with a lot of hazardous materials. Because these materials are so dangerous, we store them in this locked area. Only trained employees have the key to get in the restricted area.
    N: restricted area
2. W: We lock up the chemicals that give off poisonous fumes. Use those chemicals only in the open air. It's dangerous to breathe in poisonous fumes.
    N: poisonous fumes
3. W: We also keep flammable liquids here. Those are liquids that could catch fire easily. Of course, there's no smoking near flammable liquids.
    N: flammable liquids
4. W: There are also radioactive materials in the area. You should make sure you don't open any containers with the *radioactive materials* symbol.
    N: radioactive materials
5. W: Containers with corrosive chemicals are stored here, too. These chemicals can burn your skin if you touch them, so be careful if you work with corrosive chemicals.
    N: corrosive chemicals
6. W: Look at that fan. It has a frayed cord. An electrical fire can be caused by a frayed cord.
    N: frayed cord
7. W: There's a broken ladder over there. We need to put a sign on it. No one should ever use a broken ladder.
    N: broken ladder
8. W: Do you see that yellow warning sign? Always put one out if there's water on the floor. We always need to warn people when there's a slippery floor.
    N: slippery floor

Pg. 66   Lesson 3—Exercise 3

1. There's an electrical fire. We've got to call 911.
2. The reporter said a tornado is heading our way. We must evacuate the area.
3. The tornado might come close to the school. The children have got to go to the basement.
4. There's a major hurricane coming. Residents must leave the area.
5. Last year, there were three big storms, but it wasn't necessary for people to leave the area.
6. To prepare for the storm, it was necessary for most people to buy emergency supplies.

Pg. 67   Lesson 4—Exercise 1A

W = Woman, J = Mr. Jenks, M = Man
1. W: Excuse me, Mr. Jenks. I want to report a problem in the basement.
    J: OK. What's wrong?
    W: There are some flammable chemicals too close to the furnace.
    J: You're right. We shouldn't have put

them there. I'll get someone to move them. Thanks for letting me know.

W: No problem.

2. M: Excuse me, Mr. Jenks. I noticed a problem in the basement.

J: Really? What is it?

M: There's a spill near the oil containers.

J: Thanks for bringing this to my attention. I'll call maintenance.

Pg. 69 Lesson 4—Exercise 4B

W = Wally, A = Amelia

W: People talk a lot about the most dangerous jobs. But you don't hear much about the jobs that are the safest. Which jobs do you think are the safest? Let's go to Amelia Holt for a story on jobs that will keep you safe.

A: Thanks, Wally. When you think of safe jobs you might think of jobs in education, like teachers and librarians. And it's true that these jobs are pretty safe compared to many others. For example, in one year people working in educational services had an injury rate of just 2,440. Compare this with over 10,000 injuries for workers in the hospitality industry, places like hotels and other vacation facilities. But the safest workers in the United States work in the telecommunications industry. They have only 150 injuries and illnesses for every 10,000 workers. The computer industry is also very safe, with just 220 injuries or illnesses for every 10,000 workers. The reason for this may be that these people work in a very clean environment. They also wear protective clothing and work slowly and carefully. For other safe jobs, think about scientists with only 400 injuries or illnesses per 10,000 and veterinarians with just 680. Maybe those dogs and cats aren't that dangerous after all!

UNIT 6: Getting Ahead

Pg. 74 Lesson 1—Exercise 1C

W = Woman, N = Narrator

W: Good interpersonal skills are important in every part of my life.

1. W: I like my job, and I like my boss. He's friendly, and he likes to hear new ideas. He likes it when people make suggestions.

N: make suggestions

2. W: He listens carefully. If he doesn't understand what you mean, he'll always ask for clarification.

N: ask for clarification

3. W: I volunteer at the community parks, and people often tell me, "You're a good team player." I know that means they like the way I work in a group. It's important to be able to work on a team.

N: work on a team

4. W: When I help out at the community parks, I look for ways to make our work easier. I like to solve problems.

N: solve problems

5. W: I'm a mother, too, and of course my children disagree sometimes. I try to help my kids

calm down, and I try not to get angry. It's important to know how to manage conflict.

N: manage conflict

6. W: I always ask my kids to help find a solution when there's a problem between them. That's how I help them resolve disagreements.

N: resolve disagreements

7. W: I'm a student, too—I'm learning to paint. My teacher is great. When I ask him to look at my work, he always gives feedback.

N: give feedback

8. W: When my art teacher gives me feedback, I try to respond. I let him know that I will follow his suggestions when I respond to his feedback.

N: respond to feedback

W: I think these interpersonal skills are really important, and I try to use them every day no matter where I am.

Pg. 80 Lesson 3—Exercise 3A

W1 = Woman 1, M1 = Man 1, M2 = Man 2, W2 = Woman 2

1. W1: What kind of people do you need?

M1: We're looking for people that can manage conflict.

2. M2: Why are you changing your security systems?

W2: We need systems that are reliable.

3. M1: How was the new employee's evaluation?

W1: She got an evaluation which was very positive.

4. W2: What kind of people does the company need?

M1: We're hiring people who work well on a team.

5. W1: What is the most important personal quality for this job?

M1: The person that gets the job must be reliable.

6. W2: Who are you going to interview?

M1: We'll interview the applicants who have the right experience.

Pg. 81 Lesson 4—Exercise 1A

M1 = Man 1, Ma = Marta, M2 = Man 2, J = Jamal

1. M1: Hey, Marta. What's wrong?

Ma: There's a problem with my schedule. Who do I talk to about it?

M1: The warehouse manager. She's the person who takes care of schedules.

Ma: Oh yeah. She's the one whose office is upstairs. Do I need an appointment?

M1: Nope. Just go to her office. That's the way it works.

Ma: OK. Thanks for the help. I'll see you later.

2. M2: What's the matter, Jamal?

J: I don't understand this benefits memo. What should I do about it?

M2: You need to talk to someone in the human resources office.

J: Do I go to the manager?

M2: No, no. Mr. Gupta, the benefits officer, sent that memo. See him.

J: Mr. Gupta? Who's he?

M2: He's the man whose office is next to Accounting. You've got to make an appointment with him.

J: I'll do that. Thanks for your help.

M2: No problem.

Pg. 83 Lesson 4—Exercise 4B

You have reached Martinez Electronics. Please listen to the menu of options, and then dial the extension you need. You may dial the extension at any time.

1. If you are interested in buying a new or used computer, please dial our sales and service department at extension 111.
2. If you are calling about a computer repair, please dial our customer service department at extension 222.
3. If you are a business customer, please dial our business services department at extension 417.
4. To be connected to the warehouse, please dial extension 700.
5. For employee issues, including payroll, please dial the human resources office at extension 389.
6. For all other questions, please call our main office at extension 555.

UNIT 7: Buy Now, Pay Later

Pg. 88 Lesson 1—Exercise 1C

R = Roberto, J = Julia, N = Narrator
R: Julia and I have been renting our apartment for 6 years. Lately, we've been talking about buying a house. We know it won't be easy, but we want to try.
1. R: First, we made a list of all our assets: everything we own, including our bank accounts and our car. We have about $5,000 in assets.
   N: assets
2. J: Next, we made a list of our debts. Debts are the things we owe money on like the loans we have and the money we owe on our credit card. We have about $4,000 in debts.
   N: debts
3. R: We have an insurance policy on the things in our apartment. If there's a fire, for example, the insurance will help us replace our things. If we buy a house, we have to get a different insurance policy.
   N: insurance policy
4. J: Next, we went to State Bank to get information about a home loan. We have to borrow the money to buy a house. We got this brochure about getting a home loan.
   N: home loan
5. R: We've also been thinking about getting a new car. To buy a new car, we would need to get an auto loan, so we also picked up a brochure about getting an auto loan.
   N: auto loan
6. J: They make it look pretty easy and their interest rates are only 3.3 percent, depending on the kind of loan you get. We will decide based on the interest rate.
   N: interest rate
   R: Now we're going to look at how we're spending the rest of our money. We may need to cut our spending to afford a house. But it's worth it!

Pg. 94 Lesson 3—Exercise 3

1. If I had a credit card, I wouldn't have to carry cash.
2. If I didn't use my credit card, I would spend less money.

3. I love movies. I would rent a movie every night if I didn't have to study.
4. Not me. If I didn't have to study, I would save my money and get some sleep!

Pg. 95 Lesson 4—Exercise 1A

R = Roberto, J = Julia
1. R: Where does the money go? We'll never be able to afford a house!
   J: Sure we will. There are plenty of ways we can cut back on our spending.
   R: Well, that sounds good, but how do we do it?
   J: Well, for example, right now we spend about $300 a month on food. I bet we could cut that to $200 if we compared prices more carefully.
   R: Hmmm... Let's compromise. How about if we made it $250? Then we'd still be able to buy fresh fruit and vegetables—those are a little more expensive.
   J: OK. It's a deal.
2. J: What do you think we should spend on entertainment? $50 a month?
   R: I think that's too high. How about $20? We could rent about 5 movies a month for $20.
   J: Let's compromise. $25, and we get the videos from the library. They're cheaper there.
   R: Good idea. Even if we were millionaires, I'd still love the library.

Pg. 97 Lesson 4—Exercise 4B

O = Ms. Ogun, M = Mr. Moreno
O: Good morning, Mr. Moreno. I'm Ms. Ogun. How are you today?
M: I'm fine, but I'm afraid my finances need a little help. I decided I needed to see a financial planner, and a friend recommended you.
O: Wonderful. So tell me what's going on.
M: Well, the main problem is my debt. I thought that if I made the minimum payment on my credit card each month, I'd be OK. But the total keeps growing.
O: Yes, credit cards can be a problem if you're not careful. Tell me, what's your total debt?
M: About $5,000.
O: OK. Let's look at your monthly expenses and see where you can save.
M: Here's a list I've made. I spend about $400 a month on food. That includes about $5 a day for lunch at work. My car costs me about $250. And then I spend about $75 a month on entertainment, including cable TV. My phone bill is pretty high, too. I call my family in Honduras a lot.
O: Well, first I think you should start taking your lunch to work. If you did, you'd save at least $3 a day. You should also look for a better calling plan. You could probably save $20 a month that way. And how much do you think you'd save if you got a different cable plan?
M: At least $20 a month... You know, these are all good ideas, but it doesn't sound like I'd save that much.
O: Actually, all together you'd save almost $1,000 a year. And if you got a low-interest loan and paid off your credit-card debt with it, your monthly payments would go down and you'd save even more.
M: That's a great idea. Thanks.

O: You're welcome. Oh, and one more thing. If I were you, I'd put my credit cards away and stop using them for a year.

UNIT 8: Satisfaction Guaranteed

Pg. 102 Lesson 1—Exercise 1C

E = Vince Elko, N = Narrator

E: Good evening, viewers! I'm Vince Elko, your consumer reporter. How do you like to shop? Do you like big stores, small stores, brand new malls, or little neighborhood stores? Or would you rather not go to a store at all? Here's a look at some of the most popular ways to shop today.

1. E: The first rule of smart shopping is to look for items on sale. Today I was watching TV, and I saw this fantastic cookware on sale. The original price was $199.95, but today only they were offering the cookware on sale for $89.95. That's a savings of $110! It pays to shop when things are on sale.

   N: on sale

2. E: Of course, I was watching a TV shopping network. There are lots of shopping possibilities on TV. You see the items on TV and buy them by calling the TV shopping network.

   N: TV shopping network

3. M: Another option is an online store. You can choose items on the store's website and place an order without talking to anyone. You can shop 24 hours a day if you go to an online store.

   N: online store

4. E: Catalogs are another really convenient way to shop. You can call the company to order what you want, and they send the items to you. You can also mail in your catalog order—it just takes a little longer. If you like to shop by phone (or by mail), it's great to use a catalog.

   N: catalog

5. E: You can save money if you shop at thrift stores. These stores carry used items, things people don't want anymore. You can get clothes and furniture at really good prices if you shop at a thrift store.

   N: thrift store

6. E: You have to pay attention, though, because thrift store items are sold "as is." For example, this arm chair is being sold "as is" for $10. It has a broken arm and the fabric is torn. You won't pay much for this chair, but you can't complain about it or return it because you've bought it "as is."

   N: as is

7. E: Another great way to save when you shop is to look for items "on clearance." These items are put on sale for a very low price. For example, this old dresser has been in the thrift store for two years. The store owners wanted to sell it quickly, so they put it on clearance for only $25.

   N: on clearance

8. E: You can also shop at yard sales if you like saving money. Families sell things they don't need anymore—usually at really good prices—at a yard sale.

   N: yard sale

9. E: Then there are flea markets. These are usually outdoors, and sellers have clothes, toys, tools—just about anything you might need. You can find really interesting things at a flea market.

   N: flea market

   E: There are a lot of choices out there, consumers. Remember, it's your money, so spend it carefully. This is Vince Elko, for consumer news.

Pg. 108 Lesson 3—Exercise 3

1. Thank you for shopping at our new store today. How was your shopping experience?

2. Hmmm…Well, was it easy to find the things you wanted?

3. What did you think of the food department?

4. Oh, that's too bad. Well, what did your children think about our kids' play area?

5. Did you know that we have free babysitting while you shop?

6. I'd like to give you this application for a store credit card.

Pg. 109 Lesson 4—Exercise 1A

T = Tara, C1 = Customer 1, C2 = Customer 2

1. T: Carry-Time Luggage. Tara speaking. How may I help you?

   C1: Yes, I'm interested in ordering a blue backpack.

   T: All right. Do you have the item number?

   C1: Yes, I do. It's CP 600–14—the blue one.

   T: CP 600–14? I'm sorry, sir, but that model is sold out.

   C1: They're sold out?

   T: Yes, I'm afraid so. They're all gone. Would you be interested in brown?

   C1: No, thanks. I really wanted that one.

   T: I understand.

2. T: Carry-Time Luggage. This is Tara. May I help you?

   C2: Yes, I'd like to order backpack TC 10–560. Is it still on sale?

   T: I'm afraid not. The sale ended last week.

   C2: Oh, that's disappointing.

   T: The backpack is still available, but at the regular price.

   C2: Well, I'll think about it and maybe I'll call you back.

   T: Certainly, ma'am. And have a good day.

Pg. 111 Lesson 4—Exercise 4B

M = Meg, S = Bill Seagrove

M: Time Tone Electronics. Meg speaking. How can I help you?

S: Hi. My name is Bill Seagrove. I'm calling about a problem with a watch I ordered from you. I'm very unhappy with it.

M: OK, sir. What's wrong?

S: Well, the ad said that it would look like new for 10 years, and the glass is already scratched.

M: I'm sorry. When did you receive it?

S: I've had it for three weeks. I'm so disappointed that I just want to return it.

M: I understand. Would you like another one?

S: No, thanks. I'd just like to get a refund. What do I need to do?

M: Let me look up your order so I can give you an RA number.

S: What's that?

M: It stands for *Return Authorization*. You just need to write the RA number on your return slip and then send it to us... Your number is 14-603-4.

S: OK. Thanks for your help.

UNIT 9: Take Care!

Pg. 116 Lesson 1—Exercise 1C

J = Althea Jones, N = Narrator

J: My name is Althea Jones. I turned 101 years old yesterday! A reporter interviewed me for the newspaper. Everyone wants to know my secrets for a long life.

1. J: Heredity is one of the reasons for my long life. My great-grandmother was 94 years old when I was born. In fact, most of the women in my family have had long lives. I'm grateful for that kind of heredity.

   N: heredity

2. J: I have seen the doctor for a checkup every year. My doctor says it's important to have yearly physicals.

   N: yearly physicals

3. J: Since I was young, I have seen the dentist every six months. I still have all my teeth! That's because I get regular dental checkups.

   N: dental checkups

4. J: I had five children. All of my babies were healthy and strong. When I was pregnant, I saw a doctor every month for prenatal care.

   N: prenatal care

5. J: I have always looked for small health problems early so they don't become big problems later on. One key to staying healthy is early detection.

   N: early detection

6. J: I have medical tests done every year to make sure that I don't have any big health problems. My doctor can see if a problem is starting with these medical screenings.

   N: medical screenings

7. J: I have also been active. I loved to swim, and I played tennis until I was in my 80s. I don't watch TV, and I take a walk every day. I still have an active lifestyle.

   N: active lifestyle

8. J: I don't eat a lot of meat, and I have fresh vegetables every day. I've always believed in good nutrition.

   N: good nutrition

   J: I hope everyone reads my advice about leading a healthier life and preventing health problems. I'd like you to live to be 101, too!

Pg. 122 Lesson 3—Exercise 3

1A. You've got to start taking better care of your teeth.

1B. You should start taking a little better care of your teeth.

2A. You ought to make an appointment to see the dentist soon.

2B. You have to make an appointment to see the dentist soon.

3A. You should choose a pediatrician even before your baby is born.

3B. You must choose a pediatrician for your baby before your baby is born.

4A. You'd better ask your doctor to recommend a good pediatrician.

4B. You should ask your doctor to recommend a good pediatrician.

5A. You shouldn't wait too long before you call the doctor.

5B. You'd better not wait too long before you call the doctor.

6A. You've got to get medical screenings if your doctor thinks they're important.

6B. You'd better get medical screenings if your doctor thinks they're important.

Pg. 123 Lesson 4—Exercise 1A

D = Doctor, P1 = Patient 1, P2 = Patient 2

1. D: Have you made any changes in your lifestyle since the last time I saw you?

   P1: I'm trying to pay more attention to good nutrition. I want to live to be 100.

   D: That's a great idea. What changes have you made in your diet?

   P1: Well, I'm eating more dark green vegetables and more fruit.

   D: That sounds good. You might want to try to get more exercise, too.

   P1: I knew you were going to say that! I don't like running, though.

   D: You could try swimming or an aerobics class at the gym.

   P1: So I need to eat well and get more exercise.

   D: That's right. And get regular checkups, of course.

2. D: Do you have any health concerns you'd like to talk about?

   P2: Yes, I do. My family has a history of heart trouble, so I'm trying to keep myself healthy and in good shape. Last week, I started to take an exercise class.

   D: That sounds like a good idea. What about your diet?

   P2: Yeah... I'm cutting out fatty foods. No more donuts for me!

   D: That's smart. Cutting back on salt would be good too. What about stress?

   P2: Now, that's a problem. I need to relax more.

   D: Well, exercise helps, and you could try spending more time doing the things you enjoy.

   P2: So I'm supposed to keep exercising, try to relax, and cut back on salt.

   D: Right. Those are great steps to take.

Pg. 124 Lesson 4—Exercise 3B

1. insurance
2. serving
3. stomach
4. each
5. change
6. chronic

D = Doctor, G = Mr. Gomez
D: So, Mr. Gomez, you cut your hand working
    in your garden. It doesn't look too bad. I'll
    clean it up and put a bandage on it.
G: I don't need stitches?
D: Not this time. You'll have to keep the cut clean.
    I'll give you an antibiotic ointment to put on it.
G: Will I need a prescription for antibiotic pills?
D: No, you just need the ointment. By the way,
    when was the last time you had a tetanus shot?
G: I can't remember. I don't think I've
    had one in at least 20 years.
D: Well, you'll need to have a tetanus shot.
    Actually, since you're over 50 years old,
    you should consider having a flu shot, too.
    It's a good idea at this time of year.
G: Two shots in one day? I really
    don't like getting shots.
D: Well, let's see… You'll need to come back in a week
    so I can take a look at your hand again. I can give
    you the flu shot then. Call me if you have any
    problems, and don't forget to make an appointment
    for next week. I'll have the flu vaccine ready.
G: Great…

UNIT 10: Get Involved

M1 = Man 1, M2 = Man 2, N = Narrator
    M1: Riverview is a great city to live in. But there are
        some things I think could be better. I'm just
        one person; is there really anything I can do?
1. M2: Sure there is. Last year, for example, a group
        of us identified a problem. We were sick of
        seeing all the garbage in that empty lot on
        the corner. It really was a problem because
        the garbage attracted a lot of rats. That
        was the first step — identify a problem.
    N: identify a problem
2. M2: We stood in that lot and tried to think of
        ways to make it a good community resource.
        Maribel proposed a great solution—a new
        playground. You can't just talk about the
        problem. You have to propose a solution.
    N: propose a solution
3. M2: After that, we formed a committee to
        talk about what we wanted to do. We
        came up with a lot of good ideas once
        we started to discuss the issue.
    N: discuss the issue
4. M2: We talked about budgets and the
        kind of equipment we wanted. We
        knew we had to develop a plan.
    N: develop a plan
5. M2: Of course, we couldn't just start to build
        a playground on city property without
        permission. We needed to get approval
        and we needed money! So we took our
        plan to the city council to get approval.
    N: get approval
6. M2: Then the real work started. We agreed that
        the community would work together to build

the playground. It was a lot of fun and a
lot of hard work to implement the plan.
  N: implement the plan
  M1: That sounds like the kind of thing I could
      get involved in. I guess you're right; one
      person really can make a difference!

1. Could you tell me when the next public
    works committee meeting is?
2. Do you know why the law clinic is closed?
3. Could you tell me who I talk to
    about child care services?
4. Do you know if your city has any senior centers?
5. Do you have any idea where the city manager went?
6. Can you tell me if the public safety
    committee discussed my idea yet?

C = Clerk, O = Geraldo Ochoa, M = Olive Martin
1. C: City Clerk's office. Can I help you?
    O: Hi. This is Geraldo Ochoa. I'm calling because I
        heard that they want to build apartments near
        the park. Can you tell me if that's the case?
    C: Yes, it is.
    O: Why would they do that? It's a beautiful park.
    C: I hear what you're saying. You know,
        there's a meeting about it next Tuesday,
        at 7 p.m., in the Council Chamber.
    O: Hmmm… I can't remember where that is.
    C: It's in the Municipal Building, at 440 State Street.
    O: I'll try to be there.
2. C: City Clerk's office. How may I direct your call?
    M: Hi. This is Olive Martin. I'm calling because I
        understand that the mayor wants to cut the
        Summer Jobs for Teens program. Is that true?
    C: Yes, that's right. There is a budget cut planned.
    M: Why would the mayor cut that program?
        It's really important to the community.
    C: I know what you mean. If you're
        interested, there's going to be a public
        hearing on it at 7 p.m., in the Council
        Chamber, on November 28th.
    M: Really? I'd like to go, but I'm
        not sure when that is.
    C: It's on Thursday night.
    M: Great. I'll be there. Thanks.

A public hearing on the annual budget for the city of
East Port will be held Tuesday, March 23, at 7 p.m., at
city hall. The hearing is open to the public.

City hall is located at 1400 Washington Street. To get
to city hall, take the F4 bus to 14th Street. The bus
stops in front of city hall.

Parking is available in the public parking lot on 15th
Street. Go straight one block to Beech Street, and turn
right into the lot.

The hearing will be held in the Hearing Room. Take the
elevator or the stairs to the second floor.

Follow the signs to the Hearing Room. It will be on
your right, after Room 210.

UNIT 11: Find It on the Net

Pg. 144   Lesson 1—Exercise 1C

W = Woman, N = Narrator

W: I've been trying to find a new apartment in Chicago, and it isn't easy. But I found this great website that really helps.

1. W: Type www.rentalhomes.rent in the URL box. The address of the website or webpage always goes in the URL box.
   N: URL box
2. W: OK, now we're on the webpage. The site is called rentalhomes.rent and it's free. When you go to this website, you start on this webpage.
   N: webpage
3. W: You can search quickly through all the information on the website to find the kind of apartment or house you want. So for example, you can type *one-bedroom* in the search box.
   N: search box
4. W: To start typing in the box, click in the box. You'll see a flashing line that goes on and off. That's the cursor. You can start typing when you see the cursor.
   N: cursor
5. W: Over here on the left, there are links for information about finding a roommate or a mover, renting a truck—things like that. To get more information, you can click on the links.
   N: links
6. W: Watch out for pop-up ads. They're advertisements, usually trying to sell you something. I hate them. You can click on the X at the top of the ad to close a pop-up ad.
   N: pop-up ad
7. W: The site has apartments all over the country. To tell the site which state you want to look at, you use a pull-down menu.
   N: pull-down menu
8. W: Over on the right, you can use the scroll bar to scroll down the menu to find a state. To see the last state, move down the box in the scroll bar.
   N: scroll bar
9. W: See that little white arrow on the page? That's the pointer. Point it to the state you want and click. Sometimes instead of an arrow, you'll see a little hand. That's also the pointer.
   N: pointer
   W: Well, that's how it works. And I found a great apartment! Isn't the Internet amazing?

Pg. 150   Lesson 3—Exercise 3

1. You're from a big city,…
2. You speak several languages,…
3. You didn't go to school here last year,…
4. This isn't your first English class,…
5. Ms. Coolidge is the computer teacher,…
6. Her students don't like to leave her class,…
7. They're making webpages,…
8. We wanted to take her class,…
9. It didn't take a lot of time to learn to use the Internet,…

Pg. 151   Lesson 4—Exercise 1A

A = Abby, L = Leo

A: Leo, you're still going to help me send an email, aren't you?
L: Yes, of course, Abby. First double click on the mail icon—that's the envelope on your menu bar.
A: Double click?
L: That means put your pointer on the icon and click twice quickly. That opens your email program. Now click on *new* in the menu.
A: Like this?
L: Yes, that's good. Now, see the blank email? Click in the *To* window and type in the landlord's email address. Then click in the *Subject* window and type *Repairs for Apartment 105*. Now you're ready to write. Just click here and start.
A: So, I click here and start typing?
L: Yes, but can I suggest something?
A: Sure.
L: Make the email short. State the problem and what you want the landlord to do. Ask him to call you as soon as he gets the email.
A: That's a great idea.

A: OK, I've typed in the address and the subject. Now I can send it, can't I?
L: Yep. Click on the send button, and that's it.
A: Click on the what?
L: The *send* button, up there at the top left.
A: Oh, OK. There we go.
L: Can I make another suggestion?
A: Well sure. Please do.
L: If you don't hear back from the landlord today, send another email tomorrow.
A: That's a good idea. I need to get my heat turned on.

Pg. 152   Lesson 4—Exercise 3B

1. You know how to do this, don't you? (rising intonation in tag question)
2. You don't know how to do this, do you? (falling intonation in tag question)
3. That was a good suggestion, wasn't it? (falling intonation in tag question)
4. We looked at this website last week, didn't we? (rising intonation in tag question)
5. You're going with me, aren't you? (rising intonation in tag question)
6. He's an expert with technology, isn't he? (falling intonation in tag question)

Pg. 153   Lesson 4—Exercise 4B

L = Larry, talk show host, P = Melia Pappas

L: Our guest today is Melia Pappas, founder of the apartment finder website ApartmentSearch.apt. Welcome, Melia.
P: Thanks, Larry.
L: Tell us how you got started in the website business.
P: Well, I worked at an apartment rental office when I was in…
L: Sorry. When you were where?
P: In college. I learned a lot about the questions people ask when they're looking for apartments.

L: What is the most common question people ask?

P: Most people want to know what the landlord's responsibilities are. For example, does he have to fix things like the heat and the plumbing? Anyway, then a couple of years ago, I took a class on making your own website, and I loved it.

L: It's hard to learn to design a website, isn't it?

P: No, it isn't. It's pretty easy, but it does take a lot of time. It took me about six months to design ApartmentSearch.apt.

L: Sorry. About how long?

P: About six months. It was a big project.

L: I can imagine. A lot of people use your site, don't they?...

P: They sure do. We get... of visitors every day.

L: You get how many?

P: Hundreds. People like being able to look for an apartment or a house without going outside.

L: All right. Thanks, Melia Pappas, for being our guest today. Come back and talk with us again soon.

P: I will, Larry. Thank you for having me.

UNIT 12: How did I do?

Pg. 158 Lesson 1—Exercise 1C

K = Katie, newspaper reporter, M = Elio Moya

K: Thanks for letting me interview you, Mr. Moya. The school paper wants a story on your achievements.

M: No problem, Katie. It's a pleasure to be interviewed by someone from my old high school. In fact, I thought we'd look at a few pictures from those days.

1. K: OK, tell me about this one, Mr. Moya. I see that you're sitting on the couch with a newspaper.

M: I'm not just sitting. I'm dreaming. I had a dream of being in politics even when I was in high school. My teachers supported me. Everyone needs to have a dream.

N: have a dream.

2. K: What's this picture—what's in the letter?

M: Oh, this was when I won my scholarship. A community organization paid for my books, my college tuition, all my costs. You have to study and work very hard to win a scholarship.

N: win a scholarship

3. K: Is this a picture of your father?

M: No, that's me in front of my electronics store. I had always wanted to open a business, and when I started my business, I was very excited. It's exciting and a little frightening to start a business.

N: start a business

4. K: This is a sad picture. Your store didn't burn down, did it?

M: Yes, it did. But adversity is part of life, so I just went out and rebuilt my store. If you want to succeed, you have to be prepared to overcome adversity.

N: overcome adversity

5. K: You were really happy when this picture was taken, weren't you?

M: Happy? I was ecstatic! This was the day I lived my dream. I had become the mayor. It was a long road, but I managed to achieve my goal.

N: achieve a goal

6. K: I remember this picture. It was in the newspaper last week.

M: Yes, last week I was able to help out the local little league baseball team. These days my dream is to give back to the community that has given so much to me. I would not be where I am without the support the community gave me. It's time for me to give back to the community.

N: give back to the community

K: Thanks, Mr. Moya. I have all the information I need for my story.

M: You're welcome, Katie. I look forward to reading about your achievements someday.

Pg. 164 Lesson 3 Grammar—Exercise 3

M1 = Man 1, W1 = Woman 1, M2 = Man 2, M3 = Man 3, W2 = Woman 2, W3 = Woman 3

1. M1: Michael is thinking about making a career change.

2. W1: He's tired of being a waiter, and he wants to be his own boss.

3. M2: He's planning on leaving the restaurant business and starting his own company.

4. M3: He's been saving his money instead of spending it.

5. W2: Michael is nervous about making such a big change.

6. W3: He'll talk to a small business counselor before making a final decision.

Pg. 165 Lesson 4—Exercise 1A

M = Manager, K = Kim

M: You've done very well over the past six months, Kim. You're doing a great job of helping out the hotel staff, and you've learned a lot about working in a hotel.

K: Thank you for saying so.

M: In fact, I'd like to suggest taking a training class for hotel workers. Is that something you'd be interested in doing?

K: Yes, I would, very much.

M: Good. I'll take care of signing you up for the class.

K: Thank you very much.

M: There is something you need to work on, though.

K: Oh? I didn't realize anything was wrong.

M: Well, I've noticed that you're often late for work, and that makes things difficult for everyone in the hotel.

K: I understand. I'll try to do better. I'll start taking an earlier bus.

M: That would be great.

Pg. 167 Lesson 4—Exercise 4B

1. You need to begin thinking about taking more responsibility.

2. I appreciate the fact that you really care about doing a good job.

3. You must work on getting here on time.

4. Would you mind changing to the day shift? We need someone with your skills.

5. You need to start checking with the shift manager before taking a break.

6. You're doing a great job. I'm going to recommend giving you a raise.

GRAMMAR CHARTS

ACTION VERBS IN THE SIMPLE PRESENT

Statements	
I	work.
You	
He	works.
She	
It	
We	work.
You	
They	

Negative statements		
I	don't	work.
You		
He	doesn't	
She		
It		
We	don't	
You		
They		

Note
Most verbs describe actions. These verbs are called action verbs.

ACTION VERBS IN THE PRESENT CONTINUOUS

Affirmative statements	
I'm	working.
You're	
He's	
She's	
It's	
We're	
You're	
They're	

Negative statements	
I'm	not working.
You're	
He's	
She's	
It's	
We're	
You're	
They're	

NON-ACTION VERBS

Some non-action verbs		
be	like	see
believe	love	smell
dislike	mean	sound
forget	need	taste
hate	own	think
have	possess	understand
hear	remember	want
know		

Note
Use non-action verbs to describe feelings, knowledge, beliefs, and the senses. Non-action verbs are usually not used in the present continuous.

TYPES OF QUESTIONS

Yes/No questions and answers	Information questions and answers	Or questions and answers
A: Do you agree?	**A:** Who agrees with you?	**A:** Do they agree or disagree?
B: Yes, I do. OR No, I don't.	**B:** Everyone agrees with me.	**B:** They agree.

Direct information questions	Indirect information questions
When will the meeting start?	Do you know when the meeting will start?
Where is the meeting?	Could you please tell me where the meeting is?
What does the mayor want?	Do you know what the mayor wants?
What are the issues?	Do you have any idea what the issues are?
How did you find the meeting?	Can you tell me how you found the meeting?
Why did the mayor call the meeting?	Do you know why the mayor called the meeting?

Note
Indirect questions sound more polite than *Yes/No* or direct information questions.

Yes/No question with *if* or *whether*

Direct	Indirect		
Did they discuss the issue?	Can you tell me	if whether	they discussed the issue?
	Could you tell me		
	Do you know		

Tag questions and short answers with *be*

Affirmative statement	Negative tag	Agreement	Disagreement
You're good with email,	aren't you?	Yes, I am.	No, I'm not.
The landlord was here,	wasn't he?	Yes, he was.	No, he wasn't.
The heaters are old,	aren't they?	Yes, they are.	No, they're not.

Negative statement	Affirmative tag	Agreement	Disagreement
You're not good with email,	are you?	No, I'm not.	Yes, I am.
The landlord wasn't here,	was he?	No, he wasn't.	Yes, he was.
She isn't writing an email,	is she?	No, she isn't.	Yes, she is.

Notes
• Use a negative tag after an affirmative statement. Negative tags are usually contracted. Ask a negative tag question when you expect the answer to be "Yes."
• Use an affirmative tag after a negative statement. Ask an affirmative tag question when you expect the answer to be "No."

Tag questions and short answers with *do* and *did*

Affirmative statement	Negative tag	Agreement	Disagreement
The landlord fixed it,	didn't he?	Yes, he did.	No, he didn't.
The heat works today,	doesn't it?	Yes, it does.	No, it doesn't.
They sent emails,	didn't they?	Yes, they did.	No, they didn't.

Negative statement	Affirmative tag	Agreement	Disagreement
The landlord didn't fix it,	did he?	No, he didn't.	Yes, he did.
The heat doesn't work today,	does it?	No, it doesn't.	Yes, it does.
They didn't send emails,	did they?	No, they didn't.	Yes, they did.

THE PAST PASSIVE

The past passive			Notes
I	was		• The past passive uses the verbs *was/were* + the past participle. Lunch was served.
You	were		• We usually use the active voice in English. Sara served lunch.
He		taken to the hospital.	• The passive voice directs the action toward the subject.
She	was		• The active voice directs the action toward an object.
It			• In English, use the passive voice when we do not know who performed the action, when it is not important who performed the action, or when it is clear who performed the action.
We			
You	were		
They			

Yes/No questions and short answers
A: Were they taken to the hospital?
B: Yes, they were. OR **B:** No, they weren't.

Information questions and answers
A: Where were they taken?
B: They were taken to City Hospital.

REFLEXIVE PRONOUNS

Subject pronouns	Reflexive pronouns	Notes
I	myself	• Reflexive pronouns end with *–self* or *–selves*.
you	yourself	• Use a reflexive pronoun when the subject and object of the sentence refer to the same person, people, or thing. She saw herself on TV.
he	himself	
she	herself	
it	itself	• Use *by* + reflexive pronoun to say that someone or something is alone or does something without help from others. I watched TV by myself.
we	ourselves	
you	yourselves	
they	themselves	

REPORTED SPEECH

Quoted speech statements	
I	
You	
He	
She	
It	said, "Stop."
We	
You	
They	

Reported speech statements	
I	
You	
He	
She	
It	said (that) I should stop.
We	
You	
They	

Reported speech with instructions	
I	
You	
He	
She	
It	told me to stop.
We	
You	
They	

Notes

- Use reported speech to tell what someone has said or written.
- Use *said* to report a person's words.
- For quoted speech in the simple present, the reported speech is in the simple past.
- For quoted speech in the present continuous, the reported speech is in the past continuous.

Reported speech with *told* + noun or pronoun	
I	
You	
He	
She	
It	told me (that) I should stop.
We	
You	
They	

Notes

- Use an infinitive (*to* + verb or *not to* + verb) to report an instruction.
- Use *told* to report on who heard the words. Use a noun (someone's name) or an object pronoun (*me, you, her, him, us, you, them*) after *told*.

THE PAST PERFECT

Affirmative statements

I		
You		
He		
She	had worked	the day before the party.
It		
We		
You		
They		

Negative statements

I		
You		
He		
She	hadn't worked	the day before the party.
It		
We		
You		
They		

Notes

- Use *had/had not* + past participle to form the past perfect.
- Use the past perfect to show that an event happened before another event in the past. The past perfect shows the earlier event:
  When Ms. Porter interviewed Luis, she had prepared some questions.
  = First Ms. Porter prepared some questions. Then she interviewed Luis.

Yes/No questions

	I		
	you		
	he		
Had	she	worked	the day before the party?
	it		
	we		
	you		
	they		

Answers

	I			I	
	you			you	
	he			he	
Yes,	she	had.	No,	she	hadn't.
	it			it	
	we			we	
	you			you	
	they			they	

Information questions

	I		
	you		
	he		
How many days had	she	worked	before the party?
	it		
	we		
	you		
	they		

Answers

I	
You	
He	
She	had worked one day before the party.
It	
We	
You	
They	

NECESSITY

Present			Past			Note
I	have to		I			There are no past forms of *must* or *have got to* to express necessity. Use *had to* instead.
You	must		You			
He	has to		He			
She	has got to	stop.	She	had to	stop.	
It	must		It			
We	have to		We			
You	have got to		You			
They	must		They			

PAST OF *SHOULD*

Affirmative statements			Negative statements		
I			I		
You			You		
He			He		
She	should have	stopped.	She	shouldn't have	stopped.
It			It		
We			We		
You			You		
They			They		

ADJECTIVE CLAUSES

Main clause	Adjective clause after main clause		Note
I like working with people	who	work hard.	Use adjective clauses to give more information about a noun in the main clause of the sentence.
	that		
I can solve problems	that	happen in my job.	
	which		

Main clause			
	Adjective clause inside main clause		
The supervisor	who	hired me	likes my work.
	that		
The work	which	I do	is done well.
	that		

Main clause	Adjective clause with *whose*
I am the employee	whose paycheck was lost.
They are the people	whose children we saw.

Note
Adjective clauses with *whose* to show who something belongs to.

Main clause	Adjective clause with *wh-* or *if/whether*
I'm not sure	when the meeting starts.
She doesn't know	where the meeting will be held.
They have no idea	what the meeting is about.
I can't remember	if they're going to discuss the issue.
He wonders	whether they'll discuss the budget.

Note
Use a *wh-* or *if/whether* clause after certain expressions to talk about things you don't know for certain.

PRESENT UNREAL CONDITIONAL

Statements	
If clause	**Main clause**
If I worked hard,	I could get a better job.
If she got a better job,	she would have more money.
If they had more money,	they could live more comfortable lives.

Notes

- Use unreal conditionals to talk about unreal, untrue, or impossible situations.
- In unreal conditionals, the *if* clause can also come after the main clause: She would have more money if she got a better job.

Yes/No questions and short answers
A: Would you work if you didn't need the money?
B: No, I wouldn't.
A: If she wanted a better job, would she go to college?
B: Yes, she would.
A: If they had a car, would they drive to work?
B: Yes, they would.

Information questions and answers
A: Where would you work if you could work anywhere?
B: I would work at the college.
A: If you could have any car, what car would you have?
B: I would have a small car.

Note
Don't use contracted forms (*I'd, you'd, she'd, he'd, we'd, you'd, they'd*) in affirmative short answers.

Statements with *be*	
If clause	**Main clause**
If I were you,	I would ask for help.

Note
In formal speech with present unreal conditions, use were for all people (*if I were…, if you were…, if he were…, if she were…, if they were…*).

ADVERBS OF DEGREE

Least ←			→ Most or greatest
I am a little tired.	I am pretty tired.	I am really tired.	I am extremely tired.
I am somewhat tired.	I am fairly tired.	I am very tired.	

SO, SUCH, AND *THAT*

So…that, such…that, and *such a/an…that*	
The store is so popular	
The store has such low prices	that it is always crowded.
It is such a small store	

Notes

- Use *so, such, such a/an + that* to show a result.
- Use *so* with an adverb or an adjective.
- Use *such* or *such a/an* with an adjective + a singular count noun.

ADVICE

Advice and strong advice			
mild ↑	You	should shouldn't ought to	stay home today.
strong		had better had better not	
strongest ↓		have to have got to must	

Notes

- Use *should* and *ought to* to give advice. They mean the same thing.
- In the U. S., people don't usually use *ought to* in a negative statement.
- Use *had better* to give strong advice or to tell someone to do something.
- *Have got to* is as strong as *have to* and *must,* but is less formal.

Confirming advice	
So I	should stay home today.
	need to stay home today.
	am supposed to stay home today.
	have to stay home today.

GERUNDS AND INFINITIVES

Verb + gerund
She avoids exercising.
He quit exercising.
I'd consider exercising.
They feel like exercising.
I started exercising.
He'll continue exercising.
She likes exercising.
They prefer exercising.

Verb + infinitive
She decided to exercise.
He agrees to exercise.
I plan to exercise.
They need to exercise.
I started to exercise.
He'll continue to exercise.
She likes to exercise.
They prefer to exercise.

Preposition + gerund
She does a good job of solving problems.
She knows a lot about answering the phone.
She is good at taking phone messages.
She got a promotion instead of getting a raise.

Notes
• Gerunds are used after prepositions like *about, at, for, in,* instead *of,* and *to.*   • Gerunds are also used after verb phrases with prepositions: She cares about helping people.

Be + adjective + preposition + gerund
She is interested in learning about the review.
They are proud of getting raises.
We are famous for taking management classes.
I am happy about going to the class.

Note
Certain adjectives are almost always followed by a preposition.   She is interested in helping people.

Polite requests and suggestions with gerunds
I would suggest applying for a management position.
May I recommend training to help you reach your goals?
Would you mind asking for more training?

PREFIXES, SUFFIXES, AND ENDINGS

The suffix *-less*
harmless = not harmful
speechless = unable to speak
wireless = without a wire

Note
Add *–less* to some nouns to form adjectives.   *–less* usually means "without" or "not".

The suffixes *–er* and *-ee*		
Verb	Noun	Noun
employ	employer	employee
train	trainer	trainee
pay	payer	payee

Notes
• The suffix *–er* indicates the person who performs an action.   • The suffix *–ee* indicates the person who receives the result of the action.   A trainer trains a trainee.

The suffix -ous

Noun	Adjective
caution	cautious
danger	dangerous
hazard	hazardous

Note

Add –ous to some nouns to form adjectives. Note that spelling might change; for example, *caution—cautious*.

The suffixes –ed and -ing

disappointed	disappointing
interested	interesting
confused	confusing

Notes

- Adjectives ending in –ed describe a person's feelings. He was bored.
- Adjectives ending in –ing describe the cause of the feelings. The game was boring.

The suffix -ful

Noun	Adjective
help	helpful
care	careful
beauty	beautiful

Note

Add –ful to some nouns to form adjectives. Note that spelling might change; for example, *beauty—beautiful*.

The suffix -ment

Verb	Noun
agree	agreement
announce	announcement
assign	assignment

Note

Add –ment to some verbs to form nouns.

Prefixes for negative forms of adjectives

Adjective	Negative form
responsible	irresponsible
flexible	inflexible
reliable	unreliable
honest	dishonest

Note

Add the prefixes *dis-*, *in-*, *ir-*, and *un-* to some adjectives to make negative forms.

VOCABULARY LIST

INDEX

ACADEMIC SKILLS

Grammar

Graphs, Charts, Maps

Listening